GOD'S BIG TABLE

GOD'S BIG TABLE

Nurturing Children in a Diverse World

ELIZABETH F. CALDWELL

THE PILGRIM PRESS

CLEVELAND

The Pilgrim Press, 700 Prospect Avenue, Cleveland, Ohio 44115
thepilgrimpress.com
© 2011 by Elizabeth F. Caldwell

Printed in the United States of America on acid-free paper

15   14   5   4   3   2

Library of Congress Cataloging-in-Publication Data

Caldwell, Elizabeth, 1948–
    God's big table : nurturing children in a diverse world / Elizabeth F.
Caldwell.
        p. cm.
    Includes bibliographical references.
    ISBN 978-0-8298-1814-7 (alk. paper)
    1. Stepfamilies–Religious life.   2. Ethnicity—Religious aspects—
Christianity.   3. Parenting—Religious aspects—Christianity.   4. Child
rearing—Religious aspects—Christianity.   I. Title.   II. Title: Nurturing
children in a diverse world.
BV4526.3.C34 2011
248.8'45—dc22   2011003128

CONTENTS

Introduction . . . vii

ONE   God Who Invites . . . 1

TWO   Tables We Set . . . 39

THREE   Blessings . . . 61

FOUR   Table Conversations . . . 88

FIVE   Leader's Guide . . . 133

Reference List . . . 138

Resources . . . 143

INTRODUCTION

J esus loves the little children, all the children of the world. Red and yellow, black and white they are precious in God's sight, Jesus loves the little children of the world." Remember that song? You probably learned it in church school. I can't even remember the first time I sang it; seems like it was always in my repertoire. In retrospect, it was probably my first introduction to the idea of difference—everyone in the world did not look like me with my skin, my hair, my way of walking and thinking; other children might have families that were different than mine, live in homes that didn't look like mine, or eat food that I had never tasted.

This song also provided a simple yet profound theological statement: All people are important in God's eyes. And Jesus, God's own child, shows us how important we all are in God's eyes by loving every child, every one in the world. Now as an adult, as I look back and reflect on this simple song, I realize the complexity of its message—both practically and theologically. I probably learned to sing that song at church when I was a child. Then during the week, I would go to a store and see two different water fountains labeled for people of different color and wonder about why they were needed.

While I was singing that song, Ruby Bridges was walking past crowds of people seeking to prevent her from going to first grade in an all-white school in New Orleans in 1960. When we teach that song to children today we might be seeing the faces of children who are Asian or African American, or children who are adopted from Guatemala, Eastern Europe, or Africa. We might see faces of children who can't look us in the eye.

We still sing that song today and, although the world and the church have changed in so many ways, yet we are still far away from the dream. To sing or say that God loves everyone is an affirmation that we assume everyone believes. Yet we know that there is a "but." For example, consider these questions:

- God loves everyone—*but* what about those who don't know or love Jesus? What about Jews, Muslims, Buddhists? How wide and big is God's love? What is a Christian response to religious diversity? How does the church support interfaith families?

- Jesus loves all children—*but* if those children learn differently because of ADD/ADHD, autism, or Down syndrome, how is that love expressed in the ways they and their families are welcomed in the church?

- God's creation is good, all of it, every living thing—*but* when those precious teenagers realize that she or he is lesbian or gay, how far does the love of God extend to them and their families?

- Jesus loves children of every skin color—*but* we still struggle with how to live together with this difference in the church.

- In God's eyes everyone is loved and welcomed—*but* when a family with two children and two dads comes looking for a church home, how open are our doors?

And to think that these challenging questions are evoked by the affirmation of a simple children's song. In his book *Acts of Faith: The Story of an American Muslim, the Struggle for the Soul of a Generation*, Eboo Patel has reminded us of the words of the great African

American scholar W. E. B. DuBois, who one hundred years ago said that the problem of the twentieth century would be the problem of the color line. Patel writes, "I believe that the twenty-first century will be shaped by the question of the faith line." (Patel 2007, xv) By that he means, how do we learn to live together in a religiously pluralistic world? This I believe, is one of our greatest challenges today—how we get along, how we see the commonalities we share across faith traditions, yet at the same time how we represent our own faith tradition.

There is even a larger challenge for faithful Christians in the twenty-first century. I believe that our churches will be shaped by the larger question of difference. How do we learn to live with diversity in the ways that families are constituted and the ways that children learn? The faces of our congregations are being radically changed. Are we ready to consider these changes and their impact on the ways we teach and learn, the ways we worship, the ways we care for families, and the ways we are in service and mission?

In an earlier book, *Making a Home for Faith, Nurturing the Spiritual Life of Your Children,* which I wrote in 2000, I included a faith statement written by a teenager for her confirmation. After her affirmations about her beliefs about God, Jesus Christ, and the church, she concluded with this sentence: "I support the work of this church, trying to use inclusive language, and accepting gay, lesbian, and straight people to this congregation of faith." A few years after the book was published, I received an angry letter from a church member who said that I should not have used that faith statement or I should have edited it because the teenager was wrong. Basically her argument was that God does not accept gay and lesbian people nor should the church. The person went on to say that she was returning the copy of my book and would encourage others to do the same.

I think about that response and wonder how this person would respond to a question about the theology of the sacraments. Whose baptism do we recognize, affirm, and support? Whom do we welcome to the table where Jesus Christ is the host? Whom do we exclude?

The first book in this series on faith and family focused on the sacraments of baptism and communion, or the Lord's Supper: water, bread, and cup, the formative symbols for the life of faith for all Christians. We are welcomed with water into a life of faith and we are nourished at a table where all are welcome.

This book uses the imagery of the table as a metaphor for the ways our churches engage with difference and diversity. It begins with a chapter that provides biblical background for the welcoming of all God's children. We grow up with cherished stories from the Bible. Some of them we know by heart—the creation story, the Tower of Babel, stories about Jesus meeting people who were different, and the story of Pentecost when God's spirit was present. How do these stories work together to frame a biblical perspective on diversity and difference?

Chapter 2 examines the theology that supports the practice of welcome, hospitality, and inclusion. The Bible can be used to support arguments that deny hospitality to those who are not like us. When faced with those arguments, parents need help in knowing what to say to others and what to teach their children. Why do some of us have rigidly bounded tables with limited seating? And why do some of our churches have open tables where all are welcome?

We sit down at the table for a family meal and we hold hands and sing or say a blessing. It's what we do. It's our practice of faith. Chapter 3 will share stories of people whose lives are blessed with difference. How are the realities of their experiences forming and shaping church culture?

Table conversations are ways that children and youth learn how to interact with others—to tell a story, ask a question, laugh, argue, and reason. Sometimes we linger at the table long after the meal is finished because the conversation is so good. Chapter 4 will offer some metaphorical conversation starters—practical ways that churches and families can learn how to live with difference and diversity.

Chapter 5 concludes with a list of resources that support the exploration of this topic. Also included is a Leader's Guide for using this book with reading groups in the church.

The goals of this book are to address these issues:

- Why the topic of living with diversity of faith and culture is important
- Ways in which it is impacting church communities and why education for church members is essential
- Specific issues facing families who live with difference and ways churches can support them.

God does have a very big table. In my mind's eye it sits on a beautiful grassy space or on a very large street in the city. The construction of the table is a mystery. It has the ability to expand to fit the need of those who are there. It's like the story of Jesus and the feeding of the large, hungry crowd. A small lunch of two loaves of bread and five fish when taken into Jesus' hands became enough feed everyone who was there. So too with God's big table as I imagine it—as soon as anyone walks up, or rolls up in a chair, or is carried by another, the table begins to move. Place settings are added and food is replenished. Indeed it is not our table, but it is the table where Jesus Christ is the host, and so it must be very big, with many leaves, because at God's table all are invited; all are welcome. No one is excluded. Miracles still happen!

This book was able to be written because many people of faith invited me to their tables, literally and figuratively. They shared their stories, their questions, their doubts, and their affirmations of faith and hope. They all long for and work toward a world where they and their children will be welcomed and included. They are all people of deep faith whose commitments to living this faith in the world are both nurtured and supported by their congregations. I give thanks to them for the generosity of their spirit, the hospitality they have offered me, and the witness of their lives.

My hope is that this book will both support your questions and challenge your assumptions about difference and how Christians are called to live in this world with all of its incredible difference. Just as God looked over the world of her creation and pronounced it good, so too God's face smiles when we see that goodness. Our life together in this world requires that we learn how to listen, how to teach, how to repair the fractures among us—so that together persons of faith can accomplish what the prophet Micah reminds us all that God requires of us: to do justice, love kindness, and walk humbly with God.

· GOD WHO INVITES ·

Invitations used to come in the mail. You might recognize the handwriting and eagerly open the envelope to find out information about the party or the dinner or the open house to which you were invited. And you began to look forward to the event, wondering: who will be there? old friends, people I haven't met before? what kind of food will be served, what will I wear, what kind of thank-you gift shall I take? If there is an RSVP on the invitation, you called to give your response.

Today invitations come electronically on Facebook or by Evites. All the information about the party is there, even the guest list. And of course when you reply to the Evite, you can add a comment or say what you are bringing to the party in the way of food or beverage. Then you get a pop-up window that invites you to tell the other guests about yourself by responding to questions about your favorite restaurant, where you were born, or what you would do with $1,000. This information is shared with the other guests so you can get to know each other before you come to the party.

It's interesting to compare the form and style of these invitations. One is individually sent and received. The other is received communally—everyone knows who is invited, who can come, and who is unable to attend. One provides immediate response to the invitation with the click of a button; the other requires a phone call. One uses an old and more formal style of communication, and the other makes use of contemporary social networking via the Web. One invitation assumes that the host will provide everything for the party or meal, while the other welcomes the contributions of those who are invited.

YOU HAVE BEEN INVITED BY GOD TO A

Table Celebration!

Come anytime!
Food abounds and the table is long and wide.
Bring a friend and a dish or a story to share. Come and taste something new.
Come and stay as long as you can!
Come taste and see!

We live in an amazing time in the history of the world. Our neighborhoods, workplaces, schools, and even churches look much different today than they did twenty years ago. Ride the bus in a large city and listen for the different languages you hear being spoken. Walk down the aisles of your grocery store and notice what foods are on the shelves that you might not have seen twenty years ago.

Technological advances will continue to change the ways we live and communicate with our neighbors down the street and our neighbors in other parts of the world. The speed of connection and interfacing with new technology—the Internet, Wi-Fi, Blu-ray, smart phones, GPS, Wii—means we have information and entertainment instantly at our fingertips. And with the instant connectivity comes increasing intolerance with waiting, lingering, or patient abiding.

Living in the world today as people of faith requires that we rethink, relearn, reconsider the invitation, one that is always old, yet ever new. In Psalm 34:8, David invites the hearer "to taste and see that the LORD is good."

How have you experienced God's goodness? What has been most satisfying, challenging, disturbing? What new theological tastes have you acquired? Where do you struggle, what questions do you have? Of what are you most sure, "this I believe"? What are the things that you were most sure about and that now you call into question?

Struggling with questions such as these requires a kind of wrestling with beliefs and with biblical texts that have served as the foundation for faith. It's the faith work of adults to make sense of stories that have been heard from childhood and hold them up to the light of interpretation and new understandings.

Recall the story in Genesis 32 of Jacob's wrestling with God. Jacob didn't know with whom he was wrestling. When the one with whom Jacob was wrestling asked to be released, Jacob replied, "I won't let you go till you bless me." After asking the name of this one with whom he had been wrestling, Jacob realized that he had seen God "face to face."

Jacob was changed in this encounter with God. The wrestling was both physical and spiritual. So too with us when we wrestle with questions of faith, when we work to read the Bible with new eyes, when we are open to hearing familiar Bible stories with new ears: we are changed as we encounter God.

The wrestling that is most needed by people of faith today and by congregations is how we understand who God is in relation to difference—people who think differently than I do, people who look different from me, people of different faiths who believe in God in ways that are unique to their traditions. In her book *A Multitude of Blessings, A Christian Approach to Religious Diversity,* Cynthia Campbell, in a chapter titled "Many Faiths—One Family," reminds us that

> The Bible is not a book of theology in the sense of being a logical or orderly reflection on the nature of God. Nowhere does the Bible set out to 'prove' the existence of God. God is simply assumed. In fact, the Bible is primarily a narrative in which the first and most important character is God. The Bible is the story of God and God's relationship to humanity. In particular,

it is the story of God's relationship (in the Old Testament) with Israel and (in the New) with the followers of Jesus, who come to be known as the body of Christ or the church. While these two "communities" are the primary focus of God's relationship, it is clear in both testaments that these specific relationships have implications for the way we are to understand God's relationship to all creation and all peoples. (Campbell 2007, 21)

In the rest of this chapter, you'll have a chance to do some of this wrestling with passages from the Hebrew Bible and the New Testament. This kind of work with biblical texts becomes an important basis for thinking theologically about the topic of difference (chapter 2) and for ways that we hear and respond to the stories and experiences of others (chapter 3).

In his book *God's Mailbox: More Stories about Stories in the Bible,* Marc Gellman writes about the connecting threads that weave together our theology when we consider what it means to love God, love the Bible, and love people. He reminds us that if we love the Bible, we must struggle to understand what the stories mean. And he connects loving the Bible with loving God. "And if you don't love God, you won't be able to see how the Bible is—somehow, some way—*the* way God has talked to us. And if you don't love people, you won't understand that the Bible is the way people can best learn how to live together. The Bible is kind of like a pair of glasses through which I look at the world. I see our stories in its stories. I see all of us in all of them, and most of all I see God there and I see God here." (Gellman 1996, xi–xii)

The Bible provides a place to read and reflect on the story of God's evolving relationship with creation, with all humankind. And as Cynthia Campbell has reminded us, the stories we read in the Bible are especially instructive for us today as we figure out how to live with diversity in our world. The Bible does offer us a way of seeing and understanding, a lens through which we can look and see the world in all of its difference.

As you read these texts and wrestle with their meaning for you today, you'll have a chance to see and hear them from the lens of a fresh translation, The Common English Bible (CEB). This is a completely new translation of the Bible, which is being published in 2011. One hundred fifteen biblical scholars from twenty-two faith traditions worked as translators. After their work was completed, seventy-seven reading groups from congregations throughout North America read, reviewed, and responded to early drafts of this new translation. So more than five hundred people have been involved in this translation project. (Common English Bible 2011, vii) All biblical quotes used here are from the CEB.

If the Bible is a story of God, who invites humankind into relationship, then what texts are instructive for how we are to live together—with all the color and diversity imagined and created by God? Of course these texts are by no means exclusive, but are selected as ones that are teachable with children and youth, appropriate for reading and discussion at home. Several criteria are important in my selection of biblical texts:

- Stories common in our teaching and reading with children and youth
- Stories that can help in our understanding of living with diversity and difference
- Stories that can be read and heard in new ways because of recent biblical scholarship

The work with each of these texts will follow the same exegetical pattern, a careful reading of the text that addresses three questions:

1. Why is this story important for children and youth today?

2. How do we understand this story in its original cultural context? What did the original audience hear in this story? What was the story intended to teach them?

3. Why does this story matter now?

God does indeed invite us to:

1. Come to the table—it is long and wide with enough seating for everyone on God's guest list.

2. Be present at table together with friends and strangers.

3. Bring a story or food to share.

4. Be prepared to taste something new.

5. Enjoy the conversation; linger at the table.

6. Leave differently than when you came, seeing in new ways the possibilities for faithful living in the world.

COME TO THE TABLE—THERE IS SEATING FOR EVERYONE ON GOD'S GUEST LIST

We start at the beginning with a most familiar text, the one that we read to our children in preschool, the stories of creation in Genesis 1:1–2:4a and 2:4b–3:24. This story is important for children and youth today because it tells us about our beginnings. Children love to hear stories of their birth, their adoption, their life in their family. And as we grow developmentally, we also grow in our ability to understand and locate ourselves within God's story.

The stories of creation deal with issues that are timeless: "in God's image," God's blessing, the goodness of God's creation, putting humankind in charge, and resting. We can recall the stories of our lives with "Once upon a time." We can remember the stories of our lives of faith with "When God began to create the heavens and the earth."

The creation stories in Genesis reveal God's work and God's blessing, God's plan for humankind. We live in a world where difference of abilities, difference of the shapes of eyes and skin color, difference of sexual orientation, difference of class and culture, difference of language and food are always in front of us. This simple yet amazingly complex story of God's creation orients us to life in God's world.

The first story of creation takes in "the whole cosmos as viewed from the earth, while the second has a more limited, localized setting, taking place entirely within the Garden of Eden." (Hiebert 2003, 5)

Biblical scholar Terence Fretheim has written that Genesis is a "book about beginnings" and as such it "witnesses to the beginnings of God's activity in the life of the world.... God's continuing blessing and ordering work at every level is creational." (Fretheim 1994, 321)

Israel knew itself in relation to God's beginning work as Creator. God's gift of creation set the stage for the Israelites' understanding of God's redemptive work on their behalf as they sought to live as God's people. "God's work in redemption serves creation, the *entire* creation, since it reclaims a creation that labors under the deep and pervasive effects of sin." (Fretheim 1994, 325)

The literary form of the stories of creation is a narrative, one that invites the hearers or readers to consider who they are as a part of God's creation and who they are called to be as God's people. In its original context, it was a reminder to the Israelites of their beginnings, their family tree, as it were, a way to understand themselves as people who have inherited both "commands and promises" from God. (Fretheim 1994, 325) The story of creation served as an ancient GPS system, reminding them of where they have been, where they are, and where they are headed.

As the Israelites knew their sins, experienced their separation from God, the remembering and retelling of the story of creation reminded them of God's blessings and promises, "And it was good." They came to know that there was no sin, no act that could separate them from God's love. "The world continues to live and breathe because God makes a gracious, unconditional commitment to stay with the world" no matter what form of human sin takes place in the world. (Fretheim 1994, 337)

The stories of creation in Genesis are important today because we continue to struggle with our human condition. As God's creation we wrestle both with the evil that we empower in this world, either by our active participation or by our benign neglect, and with the good that we can do for and with all those living in God's world.

The stories of creation matter today because in them we get a glimpse of God's face. "Let us make humanity in our image to resemble us" (Gen. 1:26). Theodore Hiebert points out that contemporary theologians interpret this text differently than early Christians who connected the "image of God with human nature, and in particular, with the unique spiritual character of human life." According to modern theologians, "the divine image refers to the sanctity and innate worth of *all* human beings and presumes that all persons are to be treated with equal dignity." Their focus is on the whole person, not just on the soul. (Hiebert 2003, 7)

So you get an invitation to sit at God's table. Whom do you imagine it would be hardest to sit next to? Imagine that in that face, you see God's face. In interpreting this story for children, Ralph Milton has written it this way. "So God made people. People like you. And inside each one of us, God put some of the light that was there before there was anything. You have some of that light in you." (Milton 2007, 122)

BE PRESENT AT TABLE TOGETHER WITH FRIENDS AND STRANGERS

The story of the Tower of Babel found in Genesis 11:1–9 is well known to children. It is one that is usually included in Bible storybooks. The story describes God's people, who were all alike, living together and speaking the same language. Because of their desire to stay together, they decided to build a city and also a tower, which translators have interpreted as an act of pride. According to most translations, God then punishes them by confusing their language and scattering them. The world's cultural diversity, according to popular translations of the story, is God's penalty for human sin.

In writing about why this story matters today, biblical scholar and translator of Genesis Theodore Hiebert says that:

The story of the tower of Babel in Genesis 11:1–9 is one of the most important biblical statements about community: who's in it, what it's like, and what God wants it to be. It's an important statement because it is the Bible's first, foundational explanation of the origin of the human community in which we all find ourselves. It explains why and how the tiny, homogenous culture of a single family after the flood became the lavish multicultural mosaic of human society today. Yet for all of its crucial importance for the biblical view of community, it is one of the most misunderstood stories in the Bible. (Hiebert 2007)

Another way to read the story is by understanding it not as a story about a tower but one that tells about the "Origin of Languages and Cultures," a subheading for this story used in the Common English Bible. In this translation of an old and familiar story, Theodore Hiebert offers a new understanding of this important text, one that he believes is more faithful to the aim of the original storyteller.

> All people on the earth had one language and the same words. When they traveled east, they found a valley in the land of Shinar and settled there. They said to each other, "Come, let's make bricks and bake them hard." They used bricks for stones and asphalt for mortar. They said, "Come, let's build for ourselves a city and a tower with its top in the sky, and let's make a name for ourselves so that we won't be dispersed over all the earth." Then the LORD came down to see the city and the tower which the humans built. And Yahweh said, "There is now one people and they all have one language. This is what they have begun to do, and now all that they plan to do will be possible for them. Come, let's go down and mix up their language there so they won't understand each another's language. Then the LORD dispersed them from there over all of the earth, and they stopped building the city. Therefore, it is named Babel, because there the LORD mixed up the language of all the earth; and from there the LORD dispersed them over all the earth. (Gen. 11:1–9)

Hiebert points out the things that are not said by God in this story. God is not worried about the tower or the possibility that the people were planning on attacking heaven. God was not "threatened by the people's arrogance or by anything the people were doing. Nor does it say that God punished the people or that God cursed them with any suffering or hardship. All of these things that we associate with God's response have been *assumed* by interpreters as the only way God could respond to pride." (Hiebert 2007)

It's equally evident what God did notice. God saw that everyone was alike, culturally homogeneous. "God recognized that the human impulse toward identity and solidarity would, without intervention, succeed and continue to define community. So God put God's own plan into effect, introducing the cultural diversity and difference that make the world the complex, rich, and sometimes challenging place it actually is. Whereas the human plan for community aimed at sameness, God's plan for community aimed at distinctiveness, complexity, and multiformity." (Hiebert 2007)

In this new telling of the story, the people build the city and tower not as an act of arrogance, but rather to preserve their uniformity. The world's people, who all speak the same language, build the city to stay in one place and keep from being scattered across the earth. God's response, introducing new languages and dispersing the people, is not a punishment for the people's sin, but the way God intended the world to look. In this new translation, the world's cultural diversity is not a penalty God imposes on the human race but the original plan God had for the world.

I was privileged to hear and engage with my colleague's, Ted Hiebert's, important new translation of this story as he worked on it. The more I listened to what he was doing, the more convinced I became that this story could be retold in the language of children. We spent part of a summer working on a children's version of his translation.

We first retold the story and then in the form of midrash we worked to connect the story to those who hear it today. Midrash is an ancient style of rabbinic writing that allowed rabbis to fill in the gaps in biblical stories. "Grounding themselves in the biblical narrative, they retold the ancient story in light of new realities and changing conditions. Through this interpretive method they made sense of contradictions in the text, provided missing information, and made the narrative relevant to the times in which they were living." (Sasso 2007, 7)

Just as God created the earth with all of its difference—zebras and dogs, elephants and fleas, giraffes and cats, kangaroos and turtles, fish and snails, flamingos and cardinals, prairie dogs and panda bears, parrots and penguins. . . . Just as God created live oaks and magnolias, gingko trees and red maples, orange coleus and yellow snap dragons, pine trees and palm trees, purple heliotrope and white daisies, oleander and cliome, cedars and cactus, the good dark earth, cold wet snow, deep red clay and arid sand . . .

So God created human beings.

And we are all different, every one of us.

We speak English and Ojibwa, Igbo and Zulu, French and Russian, Urdu and Farsi, Telegu and Tagalog, Arabic and Hebrew, Japanese and Chinese and Korean, Spanish and Portuguese and Vietnamese, Bengali, Swahili, Evenki, Shoshonee, and Dutch.

We eat different kinds of bread: pita and sliced white, tortillas and rice cakes, naan, bagels, and injera, chapatti and cornbread, matzah and croissants, loaves that are fat and round and loaves that are long and skinny.

Sometimes we use forks, sometimes we eat with chopsticks, and we also use the best thing of all, our fingers.

We live everywhere on earth: Chicago and Tokyo, New Delhi and New York, Galway and Paraguay, Nigeria and Mongolia and Alexandria, Baghdad and Belgrade, Heidelberg and Johannesburg, Tolo and Cairo and Pueblo and Chico and Dnipropetrovs'k.

We come together to worship God in churches and synagogues, in mosques and cathedrals, in temples and Gurdwara and outside on the sacred earth God created.

The people who were building Babel had a little plan to stay together. But God had a big plan that was different. God wanted to fill the world with different languages, different people, and different ways of living.

And that's what God did. (Hiebert and Caldwell 2008)

A new translation for a new world of increasing diversity supports Christians who seek help in understanding why and how we should be living with our neighbors. This more faithful translation of the story of Babel is crucially important for children, youth, and their families to hear. This story about God's interaction with humans is the Bible's foundation story of cultural diversity, and as such it has a powerful effect on shaping our attitudes and those of our children toward our world.

BRING A STORY OR FOOD TO SHARE

Sometimes the invitation to the meal comes with the opportunity for the guest to bring something to the table such as food or drink. If you are the host of the meal, guests may call or e-mail you asking, "What can I bring?" And as host, you decide what you would like to have help with for the meal. As people come to the table and conversation begins, stories are shared by the guests and the gathering becomes a feast of food and conversation. Sharing of food and stories invites those at the table to taste something new or different, hear a story from someone else's perspective and experience.

Three stories in the Hebrew Bible invite us to consider the meaning of how we live in response to God. Elijah, the prophet, found himself in a difficult place and was challenged by God. The story of Ruth and Naomi reminds us how living with ethnic and religious diversity has always been both a challenge and an opportunity for God's people. And the words of the prophet Micah are timeless for those who work to connect their story with the story of God's work in the world. Read these stories and let them feed you.

Elijah

In 1 Kings 18–19:18 we hear the story of the prophet Elijah, who was sent by God to confront Ahab, king of Israel (869–850 BCE) who had set up an altar to serve and worship Baal rather than the God of Israel. When Elijah arrived on the scene in Israel, he predicted a drought, not something the king wanted to face in the early days of his administration. In order to test the power of Baal and that of God, a contest was arranged to find out who was real. When the priests of Baal called out, there was no voice, no answer. Elijah then called on God and God answered and the drought was ended.

After the contest on Mt. Carmel when the prophets of Baal were defeated by God, Elijah fled for his life because Jezebel, Ahab's wife, vowed to kill him. Elijah, the powerful prophet of God, who when he called on God and God answered, was now seen very differently— a man running for his life, a man who wanted to die.

Elijah ran to the wilderness outside of Beersheba and found shelter under a desert bush and cried out to God. He fell asleep and was awakened by an angel who had provided bread for him. The angel looked at Elijah and told him, "Get up! Eat something, because you have a difficult road ahead of you." Elijah got up, ate and drank, and went refreshed by that food for forty days and nights until he arrived at Horeb, God's mountain. There Elijah discovered that he was wanted by God even more than by Jezebel.

God asked him, "Why are you here, Elijah?" And after hearing the answer, Elijah was told to stand on the mountain because God was going to pass by. As Elijah waited for God to pass by, God was not in all the normal places Elijah expected: the powerful wind, the trembling earthquake, or the crackling fire, the forces of nature before which we tremble or stand in awe. No—"After the fire there was a sound. Thin. Quiet."

God was present in a sound of quiet. Elijah the prophet, a fugitive from God, met God, was fed by God's life-sustaining gifts, heard God in the silence and became a pilgrim who passed on God's mantle, who anointed in God's name. What a reversal—the transcending presence of God communicated in the powerful waiting of silence.

Ancient readers of this story would probably have picked up on the connection between Elijah's story and that of Moses. As a leader, Moses also wanted to die, to escape the leadership role God had invited him to take on with the Israelites (Num. 11:15). Like Elijah, Moses also asked to see God (Exod. 24:18).

This story would have spoken to ancient readers' situation, whether it was in their homeland or in exile. So it was a story of comfort and hope. "This narrative explores the interplay between human despair and God's call in a way that speaks to exiles of any age. God can be counted on to provide in the wilderness."(Nelson 1987, 129)

The original audience hearing this story would have been reminded about God's presence or appearance, a theophany. But in this story there is something different. "God is revealed not only through magnificent natural events but also through the lives and words of those who work and speak on behalf of God." (Harrelson 2003, 515)

This story is important for children and youth because it reveals one of God's chosen leaders, a prophet, who was very human. At times he was very brave and at other times he was very afraid and not so sure about his abilities as a leader. It is a great story to engage the imaginations of children about God's presence, God's voice, the nearness of God.

This story is important to us today because of the reminder of God's revelatory activity in the world in our lives. It reminds us to look, to be open to the spaces of thinness and quiet where God is speaking. It reminds us to look for the ways that God is working in the world through the lives of people all around us.

Two children's Bible storybooks tell the story this way:

"Elijah heard a soft, quiet whisper. God spoke to Elijah in a whisper. When Elijah heard God's voice, he felt strong enough to keep on being a prophet." (Milton 2007, 177)

"And after the fire, came a still small voice. When Elijah heard this soft voice, he wrapped his cape around his head and stood at the mouth of the cave. The voice said, 'Why are you here, Elijah?'" (Frankel 2009, 198)

Ruth and Naomi

The story of Ruth and her mother-in-law Naomi is a familiar one set in the time of the Judges and the early reign of David. Because of a famine, Naomi and her husband moved from Bethlehem to Moab and were living there with their sons when her husband died. Her sons married two Moabite women, Orpah and Ruth. After they lived there together for ten years, Naomi's sons died and the women were left alone. Needing to provide food for themselves, they began their journey back to Naomi's home in Judah. Naomi told her daughters-in-law that it was better for them to return to their homes so they could find husbands and thus have a secure and safe life. Orpah turned back but Ruth stayed with Naomi. And the text tells us about Naomi's response in Ruth 1:15–18:

> Naomi said, "See, your sister-in-law is returning to her people and to her gods. Turn back after your sister-in-law." But Ruth replied, "Don't urge me to abandon you, to turn back from following after you. For wherever you go, I will go; and wherever you stay, I shall stay. Your people will be my people, and your God will be my God. Wherever you die, I will die, and there I will be buried. Thus may the LORD do to me and more so, if even death separates me from you." When Naomi saw that Ruth was determined to go with her, she stopped speaking to her about it.

On one level this is a story about redemption and love, caring for others, *hesed*, which can be translated as loyalty or kindness. "The Hebrew term is a strong one. It refers to care or concern for another with whom one is in relationship, but care that specifically takes shape in action to rescue the other from a situation of desperate need and under circumstances in which the rescuer is uniquely qualified to do what is needed." (Sakenfeld 1999, 11)

It's also a story about the survival of two women in a culture with little provision for widows who had no family to support them. "The story tells us that Ruth's extraordinary faithfulness is the instrument God uses to 'redeem' Naomi through the birth of the child named Obed, whose descendant will be David, the ancestor of Judah's messianic line of kings." (Farmer 2003, 383)

For the original audience, this story would have challenged their understanding of ethnic barriers, that is, the warning to Israelites about having relationships with foreign neighbors such as Canaanites. Ruth was a Moabite, which was an ethnic group that Israelites had been taught both to hate and to reject at all levels of friendship. And certainly to marry one would be unforgiveable.

Biblical scholar Katharine Doob Sakenfeld suggests that the book of Ruth "might have addressed in story form the tensions arising already early in the post-exilic era between Jewish returnees from Babylon and those who had remained in the land after the fall of Jerusalem." The story of Ruth and Naomi reminds us that the challenging notion of racial exclusivity is a "perennial issue in the human community." (Sakenfeld 1999, 5)

And why does this story matter now? Why should we read it and teach it to our children and youth? In many stories in the Hebrew Bible the presence and voice of God directing God's people is explicit and dominant. In the story of Ruth and Naomi, God is active in the giving of food and in the gift of a baby to Ruth. Sakenfeld suggests that the work of God is more mysterious here, mysterious in the sense of how yeast works to change bread dough.

> God is at work through the everyday actions of faithful people seeking to manifest divine loyalty in their loyal interactions with those around them. To be sure, readers are not to shrink from attributing blessings in their lives to the work of God, indeed they should join the participants in the story of Ruth in praising and thanking God for those gifts. But at the same time, readers are invited to look for the human component in the blessings they receive, and like Ruth especially, to live in such a way that their own actions become the channel for God's blessings upon those around them." (Sakenfeld 1999, 15–16)

In the introduction to his telling of the story of Ruth and Naomi to children, Ralph Milton writes this introduction, "Two Brave Women."

> The Hebrew people sometimes thought they were the only people in the whole world that God loved. They even had laws

that said Hebrew people couldn't marry anyone except another Hebrew person. Not all people felt this way. Some felt that God loved everybody, not just the Hebrews. To show this, they like to tell the story of Ruth and Naomi. Ruth was not a Hebrew. But she became the grandmother of the greatest king the Hebrew people ever had. (Milton 2008, 220)

Micah

The prophet Micah lived and wrote in the eighth century BCE. Although his writings are directed to those living in Jerusalem, his concern for the poor and those without power were probably formed in his early life in a small village. (Sanderson 2003, 1303) He lived during the time of a divided monarchy. Israel was the Northern Kingdom and Judah was the Southern Kingdom. As a prophet, Micah believed he was called to remind the people of God's covenant with them, a covenant dating from the time of their exodus from Egypt. His book is a collection of oracles that includes both warnings of the destruction of Jerusalem and hope in God.

What can I bring? I love that question! I love the kind of entertaining where everyone shares, bringing something—food, drink, flowers. It has a way of turning a meal or a party into community. This same question—What shall we bring?—Was on the minds of people living in Jerusalem in the eighth century.

In Micah 6, worshipers in the temple are asking about the kinds of gifts that they should bring as offerings to God. Their concern was what would please God most. Should I bring a young calf or a thousand rams? The offering of gifts grew. "Should I give my firstborn child for my failure?" And the prophet reminds the people of something they have known but have forgotten. It seems they don't remember. Micah reminds them that God has taught them over and over again what is good and what God expects of them: "to do justice, love kindness, and walk humbly with your God." That is it; that is all and everything God wants them to bring!

This story is important for children and youth today because it helps us connect with a very old and yet timeless question: What does God expect of me? Or how can I live like God wants me to? Just like dinner guests who sometimes need a reminder about the time and place and what they said they would bring, so too people of faith in all times and places have needed reminders. Here in this small book from the prophet Micah, God's children living in Jerusalem are given a reminder, a heads-up as we would say today.

So Micah reminded them, again, of something so simple, so timeless, so consistent, so encompassing. All and everything God wants from us is to remember those who need our actions, our voices to speak up when things are not right or are unjust. All and everything God wants from us is to learn how to love kindness, to care for others, to remember those whom we meet, those whom we know, and those who are strangers. And all and everything God wants from us is to walk with God.

These words from the prophet Micah matter now as we think about the ways we are to live in the world. Remember Deuteronomy and the great commandment to love God with all our heart, all our soul, and all our strength. And here is a way to do that!

> You want to know how to worship me? You want to know what kinds of things you should give to me? . . . I want you to be kind and fair to everyone. I want *everyone*, not just a few, to have enough to eat. . . . Just quietly, in every little thing you do, try to live in God's way. (Milton 2007, 57)

BE PREPARED TO TASTE SOMETHING NEW

The invitation to a meal evokes curiosity about the meal. What will be served? And more importantly, will it be something I like, something familiar, or will it be something I've never tried before? And so the anticipation about the meal continues to grow. The world that children are experiencing in this second decade of the twenty-first century is so different from that of their grandparents and to some extent, their parents. Many children today are being raised with a palate open to the tastes of new and different. Many today are raised with tasting different kinds of foods—Thai, Chinese, Middle Eastern, Korean, Mexican—and at tables where naan or rice cakes or pita are served and opportunities arise for conversation about different ways we eat and the different cultures from which these foods come. And the neighbors at the nearby tables are potential conversation partners, people who may be Syrian, Korean, Mexican, Puerto Rican, Cuban, or Vietnamese. Children today are experiencing this same ethnic diversity at school. Our churches are beginning to experience the reality of this diversity as children from Korea, China, South America, or Mexico are welcomed into our faith community.

And of course there is all the religious diversity that they experience when they realize their best friend may be Catholic or Jewish, Baptist or Muslim—something that is totally different from what they are. In many places in this country, the world of children is much broader and more diverse than the world in which their parents were raised. A challenge is how we as adults begin to understand and interpret biblical texts that invite us to taste and see in new ways—to see how a favorite and familiar book like the hymnbook of the Bible, the Psalms, offers perspective on faithful living in a world of difference. This important work makes us better interpreters and conversation partners with children and youth when they ask questions like "Why are we all different?" "Did God make us different?"

We know the Psalms as the hymnbook of the early Israelite worshiping community. In terms of content, the Psalms are a mixture of praise and lament, prayers of thanksgiving, and songs that affirm trust and confidence in God. One scholar has described them as "a polyphony of song" . . . which remind readers today of the "plasticity of great texts, that is, their ability to address different contexts simultaneously." (Torre 2009, 666) They are representative both of individual and communal petitions and affirmations to God. "The Psalms are poetic discourse between Israel and God, who is said to hear and answer. . . . The Psalms present a rich cross section of speech to and about God, and in some cases include speech from God. At their heart is the conviction that God is one to whom all can speak. Countless generations have learned from these prayers, as various experiences have provided contexts for human understanding and ventures of faithfulness. Over and again, readers found their voices, as God's own voice joined the dialogue." (Craven 2003, 749)

Scholars have suggested that the Psalms can be grouped into five books. Two psalms chosen for our reading and reflection come from Book 1—Psalms 1 to 41—and are attributed to David. They offer us a snapshot of how one of God's faithful people understood and interpreted God's presence in his life and in the life of God's people.

Psalm 23

Psalm 23 is one that is in the memory bank of many adults, probably recited in the King James Version learned in childhood. Read this new translation of Psalm 23 from the Common English Bible.

Psalm 23
A Psalm of David
[1]The LORD is my shepherd.
I lack nothing.
[2]He lets me lie in grassy meadows;
He leads me to restful waters;
He keeps me alive.
[3]He guides me in proper paths, on account of his name.
[4]Even as I walk through the darkest valley,
I fear no danger, for you are with me;
your rod and your staff—they protect me.
[5]You set a table for me in the presence of my enemies.
You welcome me with gracious hospitality;
I have plenty to drink.
[6]Only goodness and faithful love will pursue me all the days of my life,
and I will dwell in the LORD's house as long as I live.

Now step back from this new translation and consider the meaning of the psalm. It's fairly easy to see how it is constructed. Verses 1–3 are like a faith statement: here is what I believe. Then right in the middle, verse 4 continues this affirmation but with the reminder that God is always present, always protecting. In verses 5–6 God is described as a gracious host at a table.

This psalm does indeed speak today just as it did to the original audience of Israelites. Hearing it or singing it reminded them of how they were to live in the world, trusting in God's presence with them, whatever they had to face. It reminded them of God's intimate connection with their lives, that God was their shepherd and God's greatest delight was in God's presence in their lives.

This psalm is important for children and youth today because it is a reminder of who God is and the invitation that God extends to us, an invitation across time and space. Notice how David describes the actions of God. David knows God as one who leads, keeps him alive, guides, and is always present and protecting. God invites him to a table where perhaps he met people who were not his friends. God welcomed him "with gracious hospitality."

This psalm matters now because it reminds us that we are not alone, ever. We are in God's hands in times when we are resting, in times when we feel afraid, in times when we are sitting with or talking to someone whom we think might not be our friend, and could possibly be an enemy. Consider sitting down with someone who thinks differently than you do, who may be Jewish or Muslim or Christian but who thinks differently than you do about issues in the world, political, ethical, or moral.

In the sharing of bread or a rice cake at tables of difference, in invoking the presence of God who is larger than our own particular understandings, we begin to live into the world of difference and diversity. And with the psalm writer, people of all faith traditions can affirm their desire to live life surrounded by the goodness and love of God, living in God's house. Surely all people of faith can make this same affirmation: "The LORD is my shepherd. I lack nothing."

Psalm 29

In teaching prayer to children and youth, we try and help them understand that it involves two things, speaking and listening. Think for a few minutes about your life of prayer. What kind of prayers do you pray—thanksgiving, intercession, confession, adoration? Praying with children at meals and at bedtime is a simple Christian practice that helps introduce them to being in God's presence. Parents sometimes don't know when and how to begin this practice just because of a lack of experience with it themselves.

Important in developing the spiritual practice of a life of prayer is the commitment to listening for God's voice, for waiting in silence. In a culture where noise and communication and nonstop lifestyle (24/7) predominate, finding space and time for quiet, for meditation, for listening becomes even more essential. Take a few minutes, find a quiet space, and read through this psalm of David. As you read, notice how the voice of the Lord is described.

Psalm 29
A Psalm of David
¹Give to the LORD, you gods!
Give to the LORD glory and strength!
²Give to the LORD the glory due his name!
Bow down to the LORD in holy majesty!
³The LORD's voice is over the waters;
the God of glory thunders;
the LORD is over the mighty waters.
⁴The LORD's voice is power;
the LORD's voice is majesty.
⁵The LORD's voice breaks cedars;
indeed, the LORD shatters the cedars of Lebanon.
⁶He makes Lebanon skip about like a calf,
Sirion like a young wild ox.
⁷The LORD's voice unleashes bolts of lightning.
⁸The LORD's voice shakes the wilderness;

the LORD shakes the wilderness of Kadesh.
⁹The LORD's voice causes deer to squirm in labor,
and hurries the mountain goats to give birth,
while everyone in his temple proclaims, "Glory!"
¹⁰The LORD sits enthroned above the floodwaters;
the LORD sits enthroned as king forever.
¹¹May the LORD give strength to his people!
May the LORD bless his people with peace!

The earliest audience for this psalm may have been worshipers in the synagogue gathered to celebrate God as king. For the Israelites living in a culture where there were other cultural traditions such as the Canaanite worship of Baal, it was important to affirm God's presence and in this case, the voice of God and the ways that voice was heard and seen in the land. In hearing or singing this psalm, they remembered not only God's power but reaffirmed God's presence with them.

I have always been intrigued with biblical texts that make reference to God's voice or God's presence. The transcendence of God is something we all know and understand. God does seem very far away, ineffable, mysterious. And yet in texts like this one, we see a human struggling with the immanent nature of God, the nearness of God as God's voice is heard.

Children and youth are curious about God. Does God look like a human? Where does God live? Does God see me and know what I do? How do I know if or when God is speaking to me. I got an e-mail from one of my students after class was over for the semester. She was just checking in with me and ended with "All is well and I have some great praise reports on how God showed up and showed out." This psalm almost reads like a report of how the author experienced God showing up and shouting out with a voice that could be heard over water, thunder, and flames of fire.

The ability to live in a religiously plural culture requires two things: strong affirmation of individual beliefs and openness to hearing the voice of the other, the stranger, the one who is different from you. In speaking with noted author Robert Coles about God's voice, one child described it this way: "God's voice is in you when you are making choices—it turns you towards the right direction." (Coles 1990, 75)

Using this psalm with children and youth could evoke discussion of questions such as: Where is God's voice heard today? As God looks out on our world and how we live together, what do you think God would most want to say to us? Have you ever heard God's voice? If so, what did God say to you? What helps you listen for God?

ENJOY THE CONVERSATION, LINGER AT THE TABLE

You know a meal or party has been a success when conversations at the table are lively and sustained, when people are so involved in talking and listening that time passes very quickly. At gatherings, whether standing with beverage and appetizer in hand or seated around a table, friends have time to catch up with each others' lives. New faces are seen and connections are made with favorite questions like: What do you do in life? Where do you live? (or if you live in the South) Where do you go to church? Sometimes e-mail addresses are exchanged or the question, "Are you on Facebook?" And social networking begins.

There is a certain level of comfort involved when we are in charge of the guest list and know who the conversation partners will be. And then there is the interesting challenge of going to a party where you don't know all the other guests and you realize you will need to work a bit harder, talking and listening to strangers, people you may or may not ever see again.

There are many ways to read the Gospels in the New Testament. You can of course read each of them from beginning to end. You can read them comparatively, noticing which stories are similar and specific to Matthew, Mark, Luke, and John. And then there is the thematic reading. One theme that I find interesting is that of "People Jesus Met." Who are some of the particular people Jesus invited into conversation and, indeed, into relationship, and how are these stories instructive for our thinking about living with diversity?

Three stories that are familiar to children and youth and ones that deserve our rethinking are the parable of the great banquet, Zaccheus, and Jesus' postresurrection encounter with the disciples on the Emmaus Road. In preparation for your own engagement with these stories, read them again.

Great Banquet (Luke 14:12–24)

From our reading of the Gospels, we know that Jesus sat at table with all kinds of people. This story in Luke tells about a time when invited guests sat down for a meal with Jesus at the home of a leader of the Pharisees. They were probably honored to have been asked to the home of this important religious leader and they also probably had no idea what would happen. Having been focused on whether or not they would be on the invitation list, they weren't prepared for Jesus' question: Whom will you invite to your table?

Jesus told them a parable about someone who planned a dinner for a lot of people. As the date drew closer for the meal, excuses started coming in. So the host opened up the invitation list: "Go out into the streets and roads of the city right now and bring the poor, crippled, lame, and blind in here."

The original audience hearing this story might have been surprised by the parable. Everyone would understand replacing the guests who couldn't come with other friends. But instead, the host sent his servant to places where his friends probably didn't live: on the streets and outskirts of town. "Jesus is not calling on Christians to provide for the needs of the poor and disabled; he says to invite them to dinner. This is the New Testament's understanding of hospitality . . . which means literally, 'love of a stranger.' . . . The clear sign of acceptance, of recognizing others as one's equals, of cementing fellowship, is breaking bread together." (Craddock 1990, 178)

This is a great story for families to read and discuss together because it addresses that space between what we say we believe and how that belief is visible in our actions. It makes a connection with the words that some pastors use at a child's baptism, reminding the congregation of their promise to nurture the child in the life of the Christian faith. "Tell this child the stories of Jesus and, if you must, use words."

"Those who embrace and embody the message of Jesus are known by their practices of hospitality to the least and the left-out." (Green 2003, 1882)

The story of Jesus dining with guests at the home of the leader of Pharisees is important today because of the questions it raises for the contemporary hearers of this story. What does it mean to be hospitable? With whom do you share meals? At soup kitchens or shelter meals, do you sit down with the guests and break bread with them? In what ways have you been blessed by sharing a meal with someone who could never return the favor?

"If you are going to do a favor for someone, like inviting them for dinner, don't do it to someone who has lots of money and a nice big house. Don't invite your friends or your family or people like that. They can invite you back. . . . Here's a better idea. Invite someone who can't invite you back. Invite somebody who is poor and who doesn't have nice clothes or a nice house. Because when you do that, God will bless you. You will make God smile." (Milton 2009, 190)

Zacchaeus (Luke 19:1–10)

Children grow up singing the song about Zacchaeus, the short tax collector who wanted to see Jesus and so he climbed up a tree so he would be able to see him in the crowd. Jesus spotted him and invited himself to Zacchaeus's house. Of course the crowd was really angry, not at all happy that Jesus would be a guest in the home of one whom they considered to be a sinner because of his position as a chief tax collector in Jericho, a job that provided him both with power and wealth in a corrupt system that left many people poor and in debt.

But something happened in this encounter with Jesus. The text doesn't provide a lot of details. Perhaps they went to his house and shared a meal together. Maybe at table, they discussed Zacchaeus's life and work and Jesus shared something of his own life and ministry. Whatever happened, Zacchaeus admitted the wrongs he had done and promised to make up for it by repaying people whom he had defrauded. And Jesus announced that salvation had come to Zacchaeus's house and reminded those around him that he had come "to seek and save the lost."

So how did the original audience hear and understand this story? What in this story contributed to their understanding of who Jesus was and what he was asking, teaching, and expecting of those who would be his disciples? In Luke 7:34, we read that Jesus was quite public with his announcement that he was a "friend of tax collectors and sinners." So here is a story about just one of those people. The telling of this story challenged those around Jesus to consider what it meant to offer hospitality to someone who was perceived to be unworthy of God's love, outside the bounds of God's family.

Luke 19:1–10 tells the story of "the salvation of a man who was rich (all things are possible with God, 18:27) and a tax collector. His life-style and the resultant treatment by community and synagogue had not moved him beyond the reach of God's seeking love." (Craddock 1990, 219) This story also opened up the concept of salvation for these first-century followers of Jesus. Zacchaeus's salvation has "personal, domestic, social, and economic dimensions. In addition, we should not forget that in other stories 'saved' is translated 'made well,' 'healed,' and 'made whole.' Luke would object to confining the word to a condition of the soul. The whole of life is affected by Jesus' ministry, a foretaste of the reign of God." (Craddock 1990, 220)

This story is still important for hearing by contemporary readers who struggle with being healed, being whole in God's eyes. Like Zacchaeus, we struggle with lifestyle, how much we need to live on, how much we have to share. "Salvation enters Zaccheus' house when he dies publicly to the power and privilege that had supported his lifestyle and is moved to act on behalf of the poor. He becomes the first character in Luke's narrative to respond to Jesus' teaching regarding wealth and poverty." (Torre 2009, 1498)

This story is important for children and youth to hear and engage and interpret in light of their own day-to-day experiences because class issues—wealth and power, poverty and exclusion are still as visible in our culture as they were in Jerico when Jesus was visiting there.

In his *Lectionary Story Bible*, Ralph Milton titles this story "Zacchaeus Finds a New Way to See." In Zacchaeus's conversation with Jesus, Milton imagines it ending this way: "Jesus took Zacchaeus's hand. 'Something very important has happened, Zacchaeus. You've just learned how to live God's way.'" (Milton 2009, 219)

Emmaus Road (Luke 24:13–35)

Sometimes when inviting worshipers to the communion table, I tell the story of the two disciples walking on the road to Emmaus with Jesus, whom they do not recognize. It was not until they sat down for the meal after the end of the journey from Jerusalem to Emmaus that they knew with whom they had been walking and talking.

Luke is unique in the way that he begins and ends his account of the life of Jesus. He closes his book with narratives of the resurrection of Jesus that focus on four stories: the empty tomb, Jesus' appearance on the road to Emmaus, his appearance in Jerusalem, and his blessing and leaving. Jesus' appearances all take place in or near Jerusalem and they are told as taking place on the first day of the week. In this way, the stories could easily be used by the early church in the celebration of Easter. (Craddock 2009, 280)

The story of Jesus' appearance on the road to Emmaus is only told in Luke's gospel. Two disciples were traveling from Jerusalem to the village of Emmaus. Their conversation focused on all that they had seen and heard about Jesus. In the midst of their conversation, Jesus arrives but "they were prevented from recognizing him" (Luke 24:16). The disciples included Jesus in their conversation and they brought him up to speed on what had happened to Jesus in Jerusalem.

In response to their details about the tomb and their friends who went there looking for Jesus but couldn't find him, Jesus began to explain to them the scriptures and how God is revealed in the life, work, death, and resurrection of Christ. As they arrived at their destination, the disciples invited Jesus to join them. They sat down for a meal.

In the offering of food and fellowship, Christ is revealed to them. "Christ had not forced himself on them, but when invited, the guest becomes the host." (Boring and Craddock 2009, 281) And using the familiar words we hear at the Lord's Supper, Christ feeds them. And Luke writes, "Their eyes were opened and they recognized him" (Luke 24:31).

Christ left them and the disciples immediately returned to Jerusalem to tell others what had happened and how they knew Jesus had risen because he "was made known to them as he broke the bread" (Luke 24:35).

For first-century Christians trying to figure out how to live as faithful followers of Jesus, this story would have helped them understand the meaning of faith in light of Jesus' resurrection. It must have been difficult for those who followed Jesus to make sense of everything they had witnessed in his teachings, his death, and the report of those who had gone to the tomb and found it empty.

Here in the account of Jesus meeting disciples on the road, Luke confirmed Christ's resurrection, making it real for them in ways the reports of the empty tomb had not been able to do. "As they worshiped together around the Lord's Table, the meaning of Christian faith and the reality of the risen Lord became real. Scripture and Eucharist were the setting and means for reinterpreting the story of Jesus, now seen in a new light." (Boring and Craddock 2009, 281)

This story is important even today for us as followers of Jesus who struggle with recognizing him. What does it take for our eyes to be opened to see people and situations in the ways that Jesus would see them? We need to tell this postresurrection story of Jesus to our children so they can connect Jesus' life and teachings with their own concrete acts on behalf of others. Telling this story also helps children and teenagers make connections between the meal we share at church and the bread we break with family and friends.

In this story, the meal is an ordinary one, not the one that Jesus served at Passover. "As in Acts, the boundary between 'ordinary' meals and the Eucharist grows thin. Every meal can point to the risen Christ." (Boring and Craddock 2009, 281) We share food with strangers, we offer help and support for those in prison, we provide shelter and clothes for those who don't have any, we fight unjust laws that dehumanize others.

We do this and our children are watching or working with us. And as they watch and help, they learn the connection between the meals at church and the meals at home that nourish and sustain us for a life of faith. At all of these tables, our eyes are opened, and we recognize him and we are able to see others.

LEAVE DIFFERENTLY THAN WHEN YOU CAME, SEEING IN NEW WAYS THE POSSIBILITIES FOR FAITHFUL LIVING IN THE WORLD

Invitations to a meal bring with them the expectations of both excellent food and engaging conversation. Over the course of breaking bread together, there is the opportunity for hearing stories, hearing about what's going on with kids, sharing titles of books being read or movies or discussion of news items, political events, or just catching up on what's going on with each others' lives. I always leave a dinner or a party with the realization that I've learned something new. Conversations at the table provide the chance for us both to share stories and to hear stories from each other.

Jesus had an encounter with a woman in Matthew that is an excellent example of how thinking and acting can change or transform a person. At first glance, the story of the faith of the Canaanite woman in Matthew 15:21–28 seems like a strange one because of the conversation she had with Jesus. He had been in Jerusalem and had left for the Gentile cities of Tyre and Sidon.

When the woman saw him she said she pleaded for mercy, help with her daughter. Jesus ignored her, and his disciples, concerned that she was bothering them, encouraged Jesus to send her away. Jesus replied, "I've been sent only to the lost sheep, the people of Israel." Rather than leaving, she persisted with her plea for help. And then Jesus replied with the comment that on the surface sounds so strange,

"It is not good to take the children's bread and toss it to the dogs." And she replied, "Yes, Lord, but even the dogs eat the crumbs that fall off their master's table." And the Gospel writer records that Jesus replied, "Woman, you have great faith." And her daughter was healed.

The story is an example of the depth of background required for engaging what on the surface appears to be a simple story of Jesus meeting one more person wanting healing. The New Interpreter's Study Bible gives you a heads-up about the complexity of this passage when in a note that introduces this story it says, "Cultural, ethnic, political, economic, and religious barriers and prejudices operate in this scene." (Carter 2003, 1774)

Jesus has left Israel and has traveled to a place different in culture and ethnicity. He is in Gentile territory and he takes with him his own cultural, ethnic, political, and religious identity. And he comes face to face with a Canaanite woman, a Gentile, someone who was not put off by his rejection of her because she was not an Israelite. "The woman is undeterred, and in the kneeling posture of Christian worship continues to address her psalm-like petition to Jesus as 'Lord.'" (Boring 1995, 336)

In Jesus' response to her, Jews are compared to children and Gentiles are compared to dogs. Rather than being offended by the comment, the woman continues to address Jesus as "Lord" and persistently pursues her request. This address to Jesus was only used by believers. Here is a mother fighting for the life of her child and she will not be deterred.

The original audience would have heard a remarkable story of a Gentile woman confronting Jesus, a Jewish man. They heard Jesus' attempt to dismiss the woman and her request. They would probably have struggled with the cultural and religious prejudices of their day. In what ways was the faith of the disciples and those who followed Jesus similar to or different from the faith of this Gentile woman? Did the disciples attempt to dismiss her because she was a woman or because she was a Gentile or both? The original audience may have wondered about these questions.

This story is important to us today as we consider the ways Christians wrestle with scripture that sheds light on living with diversity in our world. Biblical scholar Eugene Boring suggests that there are three meanings in this story that give insight to both the work of God and the meaning of faith.

First, in God's plan, we see how Jesus first offers salvation to Jews and then includes everyone, as recorded in Matthew 28:16–20. The signs of the coming of God's realm are visible in small ways in the present. "It already erupts into the present." (Boring 1995, 337) The faith of a woman evokes divine compassion on the part of Jesus. "God is not enslaved by any theology, even one announced by God's son. . . . This text springs the boundaries of theology, without breaking it or abandoning it." (Boring 1995, 337)

Notice Matthew 15:28. Jesus addresses her as a woman of great faith. Contrast this with Jesus' response to Peter in Matthew 14:31 when, terrified of the storm, Peter asks Jesus to save him. And Jesus describes him as one of "little faith," "the dialectical mixture of courage and anxiety, of hearing the word of the Lord and looking at the terror of the storm, of trust and doubt which is always an ingredient of Christian existence, even after the resurrection." (Boring 1995, 328)

The Canaanite woman had no doubt. She announced who Jesus was and asked for help. Her great faith is used by the gospel writer to provide a way for the original audience and a contemporary one to struggle with the nature of faith. "We tend to assume we know what faith is, our main problem being that we do not have enough of it." (Boring 1995, 337)

And finally this short encounter of Jesus with a Gentile woman raises questions and assumptions that we share with those in the original audience who heard this story. It challenges "the sexism and racism of readers, ancient and modern, who tend not only to consider those of different gender and ethnicity as 'the other,' somehow more distant from God and the divine order and plan than our own group. . . . The story invites readers to place themselves in the role of the other, to struggle not only with God but also with our own perceptions of the other, and pronounces such enduring struggle to be great faith." (Boring 1995, 338)

This story is an important one for youth today. Confirmation education is often offered at a time in the life of teenagers when they may have questions about their faith, their beliefs. As they attempt to make sense of their world through the lens of their faith, this story could help them see that the responses of disciples, the woman, and Jesus reveal aspects of faith and doubt. This wrestling with biblical text could evoke an even larger discussion of God's redeeming work with all people of faith.

In his retelling of this story for children, Ralph Milton imagines what Jesus might have been thinking as he wondered how to respond to the Canaanite woman's request for recognition and for healing for her daughter. Milton imagines Jesus recalling the stories he had heard as a child of how Jonah was sent by God to the people living in Nineveh who were not Jewish; or the story about Ruth, a Moabite, who was King David's ancestor; or the story told him by his mother about three Magi who sought him out as a baby and presented him with very special gifts.

Milton writes, "'You are right,' said Jesus. His voice was just a whisper. 'Of course you are right. You are also very brave. Go home. Your daughter will get well. And thank you for coming. You've given me a lot to think about.'" (Milton 2007, 185)

The Book of Acts, attributed to the gospel writer Luke, is a great story of the early church. It describes how those who were followers of Jesus were trying to make sense of their lives after Jesus was gone, and how to make sense of the world in which they were living. In his commentary on this book, William Willimon writes, "Scripture is the story of a particular people to whom certain peculiar events occurred. . . . Something happens to us as we listen to stories like those of Acts, because each of us in our own congregations, in our own lives, is trying to tell a story in a way that makes sense." (Willimon 1988, 2)

He goes on to describe the three characteristics of stories we read in scripture. Stories like those in Acts "make sense." They have meaning and, when retold, we hear again the presence of God behind the story. "God is not just a character in the story, rather God is the author who makes the story possible and whose nature and purposes are revealed in the telling of the story." (Willimon 1988, 2)

Second, the stories in Acts are not only revelatory about who God is, but they also reveal the kind of world that is God's intention. The stories reveal the ways that God is at work, faithful to God's promises. "Therefore the future is never completely closed, finished, fixed. God has been faithful before (history) and will be faithful again (apocalyptic). The story is a stubborn refusal to keep quiet and accept the world as unalterably given." (Willimon 1988, 3)

Third, the purpose of the stories in Acts is concerned with forming and equipping those who would be disciples of Jesus. "The stories in Acts not only depict an author, God, not only render a new world, God's world, but they also render a new way of living, discipleship in the church." (Willimon 1988, 4)

Acts 2:1–13 tells the story of how the gift of God's spirit renewed and energized Christians living in community as they began to discern how they were to live in response to Jesus' life, teaching, death, and resurrection:

> The people have gathered seven weeks after Jesus' death and resurrection. This time they are again, all together in one place. But suddenly God's spirit rushed in like a huge windstorm and each one started speaking a different language. And they looked at each other wondering what it meant.

For a community of believers living on the other side of Easter, Peter's sermon on what we call Pentecost, the birth of the church, reminded them and us of God's promise. God's Spirit, the living presence of God, would pour down on them. "All of them were filled with the Holy Spirit and began to speak in other languages, as the Spirit enabled them to speak" (Acts 2:4).

Consider the variety of languages spoken in your congregation: of age, gender and sexual orientation, and political persuasion. In our churches we listen to the languages of those who are learning to speak and those whose speech has grown less certain with age and health. Our children speak the language of their birth cultures and we learn how to teach and learn by listening to differently abled kids.

When we welcome shelter guests to our church rooms we hear stories of life and and hope. When we take the time to meet and listen to those whose beliefs are different from our own, we learn about the wideness and depth of the language of faith in God's world. Just as in the story of the early church in Acts, our congregations are remarkable communities of people who love God, and we are all different. And we struggle to hear, to understand, but we do that in community, together in worship, in education, in mission.

And then Peter reminded them of the words of the prophet Joel. He concludes his speech with these words, "Then everyone who calls on the name of the Lord shall be saved." This story helped God's people remember how God was still at work in their community, how God's spirit would equip them to be God's faithful disciples. In recalling the words of the prophet Joel, Peter reminded them of the inclusive nature of God's abiding love.

It is important to teach this story to our children. It helps them know that a lot of what the early community of Christians did together—pray, share meals, worship—we still do as God's people today. Like the story of God's people living in Shinar told in Genesis 11, the early Christians living in Jerusalem were comfortable in their sameness. And with a great rush of a very strong wind, everything changed for them. They looked over their shoulder and heard languages that were different. They literally felt and saw God's Spirit present in all the different languages represented by the people who were there.

And finally this story is still important today because it illustrates a consistent and powerful theme in the Bible. If there is one story that moves across the Hebrew Bible and the New Testament, it is this:

- The story of a God of love whose breath created all life.

- The story of a God of love who wants humankind to learn how to live together.

- The story of a God who sent God's only son, Jesus, to show us how to live the story of God's spirit rushing in among us, even today, mixing it up a bit, challenging our assumptions and notions about who it is God loves.

How did we get to be so different? Why do people speak so many different languages? Wouldn't it be easier if we were all alike? Our story is like that of the people of Shinar who were building Babel and had a little plan to stay together. But God had a big plan that was different. God wanted to fill the world with different languages, different people, and different ways of living. And that's what God did. God surprised them. God surprised God's people gathered in Jerusalem on Pentecost and God is still surprising us today.

GOD'S INVITATION

I have a friend who is a photographer. When I am invited for dinner to her home, I am surrounded by Terry's photographs. She is a gifted artist and teacher of photography and her angle of vision on the world enlarges my own perspective on God's creation.

When we finish a meal, her husband, Sam, always takes a photograph of the people who are there. Sometimes these photographs appear in a slide show or they are made into a small book for a Christmas present. But they always appear in an e-mail attachment soon after the dinner. A moment of sharing food and conversations that are both light and deep, honest and challenging, are captured and remembered.

Consider recent table conversations you have had with family or friends. Perhaps it was as simple as talking with your children about their day at school and the "sads and glads" of the day. Or maybe it's a conversation with teenagers, which can be alternately hilarious or frightening, depending sometimes upon how much they want to tell you and how much you really want to know about their lives. Or maybe it's a hard conversation about something that's going on at work, school, within the family, or in the world.

In his book *Acts of Faith*, Eboo Patel tells the story of his high school lunch group, which included a Cuban Jew, a Hindu from India, and an evangelical from Nigeria. The silent pact that they had to not talk about their religious differences was a comfort to them. "We were not equipped with a language that allowed us to explain our faith to others or to ask about anyone else's. Back then, I thought little about the dangers lurking within the silence." (Patel 2007, xvii)

After graduation, one of his friends reminded him of the time when anti-Semitic comments appeared on desks and in comments in the halls. Patel remembered the incident and also recalled his lack of response to his friend or to the situation. "I did not know it in high school, but my silence was betrayal: betrayal of Islam, which calls upon Muslims to be courageous and compassionate in the face of injustice; betrayal of America, a nation that relies on its citizens to hold up the bridges of pluralism when others try to destroy them; betrayal of India, a country that has too often seen blood flow in its cities and villages when extremists target minorities and others fail to protect them." (Patel 2007, xix)

Patel never forgot that experience. As a young adult he created the Interfaith Youth Core, providing space and time for teenagers and young adults from different faith traditions to learn from and with each other through service and dialogue. "Pluralism is an intentional commitment that is imprinted through action. It requires deliberate engagement with difference, outspoken loyalty to others, and proactive protection in the breach. You have to choose to step off the faith line onto the side of pluralism, and then you have to make your voice heard." (Patel 2007, xix)

The days of carrying photographs of friends and family are very much in the past, replaced with Facebook pages, pictures on our phones, and digital drop boxes. Occasions in our lives are both instantly captured and immediately shared. Photographs invite us to remember and recall. So too God invites us into relationship. God's promises are sure and completely trustworthy. God invites us to remember God's plan for the world. God's invitation list is very long and inclusive. All are welcome at God's table.

· TABLES WE SET ·

I t's Saturday night and a family with teenage boys sits down for dinner. Friends of two of the teenagers join them for the family meal. Hands reach out for the blessing, which they have been singing together since the boys were in preschool. One of the friends has learned the blessing since he has been a regular dinner guest at this table. In explaining this to the other friend, the mother says, "It's what we do."

"It's what we do!" We say thank you to God for health and strength and food to eat. Some speak of the important role of parents in helping their children "find faith at home." I don't think the issue is really one of finding faith at home as much as it is living the faith at home. What tables of faith are we setting in our homes?

A few years ago, an article in the Sunday *New York Times* caught my eye with its intriguing title, "Coveting Luke's Faith." A mother wrote about her own lack of faith in light of watching her young son's practice of praying and she wrote about her own childhood experiences.

> When I was a child in Sunday school, I would ask searching questions like "Angels can fly up in heaven, but how do clouds hold up pianos?" and get the same puzzling response about how that was not important, what was important was that Jesus died for our sins and if we accepted him as our savior,

when we died, we would go to heaven, where we'd get everything we wanted. Some children in my class wondered why
anyone would hang on a cross with nails stuck through his
hands to help anyone else; I wondered how Santa Claus knew
what I wanted for Christmas, even though I never wrote him
a letter. Maybe he had a tape recorder hidden in every chim-
ney in the world. This literal-mindedness has stuck with me;
one result of it is that I am unable to believe in God. Most of
the other atheists I know seem to feel freed or proud of their
unbelief, as if they've cleverly refused to be sold snake oil. But
over the years, I've come to feel I'm missing out. My friends
and relatives who rely on God—the real believers, not just the
churchgoers—have an expansiveness of spirit. When they
walk along a stream, they don't just see water falling over rocks;
the sight fills them with ecstasy. They see a realm of hope beyond this world. I just see a babbling brook. I don't get the
message. My husband, who was reared in a devout Catholic
family and served as an altar boy, is also firmly grounded on
this earth. He doesn't even have the desire to believe. So other
than baptizing our son to reassure our families, we've skated
over the issue of faith. (Tierney 2004, 666)

Perhaps you know someone like this or perhaps you know someone (even yourself) who struggles with how to understand this thing
called belief and how to interpret Christian faith both to children and
grandchildren, nieces and nephews as you live in a religiously plural
world. As I read the wealth of literature on pluralism, diversity, and
religion and as I listen to adult family members with their questions
about raising children in the life of the Christian faith, four questions
come to mind.

   1. *What happens when we "skate over" the issue of faith?* For several
years, NPR had a segment called "This I Believe" that aired each
Monday. People from all walks of life wrote and read their essays on
what they believed. The essays are still archived there on the website

and also included in a book. I loved hearing the people speak about a belief that was important to them. As you can imagine, the topics were extremely varied.

In order to be able to set a table of faith at home, parents need to be able to articulate what it is they believe, both with words and with experiences. It is essential for parents to skate into the issue of faith, not over it.

2. What does it mean to be firmly committed to both your own faith tradition and to interfaith cooperation? This is a question asked by Eboo Patel, who is Muslim. As a young adult, he began the organization called Interfaith Youth Core, which works to bridge differences of culture and faith through dialogue and service. Patel comments on the hard work of religious pluralism, that it's neither different religious traditions coexisting together nor is it forcing religious communities into consensus. Rather he writes, "It is a form of proactive cooperation that affirms the identity of the constituent communities while emphasizing that the well-being of each and all depends on the health of the whole. It is the belief that the common good is best served when each community has a chance to make its unique contribution. (Patel 2007, xv)

Patel's question is important because it recognizes the place where we struggle. How can I be Christian and live with, understand, and work beside those who don't share my beliefs? Religious leaders active in the interfaith movement affirm this: "There is a way to get along, cooperate, and even respect one another while still holding firmly to one's own religious identity." (Jethani 2009) But in order to be able to be in dialogue with a Muslim, a Jew, or even one of the many Christian traditions, one must first know one's own beliefs, the commitments that support one's life of faith.

3. What are we called to question and what are we called to affirm? What are we called to reexamine, relearn, rethink, as we live into being Christian in a religiously plural culture? In her book *Called to Question: A Spiritual Memoir*, Joan Chittister writes, "We suckle ourselves on clear and comfortable answers because we fear to ask the questions that make the real difference to the quality and content of our souls. The spiritual life begins when we discover that we can only become spiritual adults when we go beyond the answers, beyond the fear of uncertainty, to that great encompassing mystery of life that is God." (Chittister 2004, 9)

Just as children grow and develop in their faith—in their understanding of God and the ways they are called to live in the world as disciples of Chris—so we, the adults in their lives, continue to grow, to ask deep questions, to wrestle with the life of faith.

As I write this, relief efforts for the survivors of the hurricane in Haiti are still ongoing. As I write this, a story in the newspaper tells about the religious fight going on between a husband and wife who are divorcing. She is Jewish and he is Catholic and both are intent on raising their child in their own faith tradition. As I write this, the mark of ashes on my forehead to mark the beginning of Lent are a fresh memory. While I drove home from that service, another family also drove home, but they did not arrive safely. A daughter whose forehead had been marked with a circle as her mother, the pastor of the church said to her, "Come full circle in the love of God," did not make it home alive that night. After a tragic car accident, this family of children and adults is left with their faith, including both strong beliefs as well as deep questions.

Life is fragile and we live in difficult days. The tables of faith we set in our communities of faith and in our homes prepare us, sustain us, and hold us when we face the challenges and questions that come our way.

4. *"In light of what we know now, what does faithfulness to God look like?"* (Forbes, 2010) Television talk show host Tavis Smiley recently interviewed James Forbes, senior minister emeritus of the Riverside Church in New York City, who is actively working to help people of differing faith traditions learn from each other through his foundation, Healing of the Nations.

James Forbes formed this question in response to Smiley's question about whether or not Jesus changes. In responding to Smiley's question about the never changing nature of Jesus, Forbes posed the question of how to contrast and compare the text in Hebrews 13:8, "Jesus Christ is the same yesterday, today, and forever!" with Luke 2:52, "Jesus matured in wisdom and years, and in favor with God and with people." In this interview, two people of faith wrestled with their beliefs, their questions, and their affirmations.

In light of what you know now, in light of what you have experienced of the Christian faith, in light of what you have observed in others, what can you say about being faithful to God? This is the question, the lifelong question that we live with all the days of our lives. How can we live in response to the waters of our baptism, waters that mark us forever for a life of faith? Who are we called to be as faithful Christians and how are we called to live in this world as ones who follow Jesus, God's beloved Son?

This chapter is an invitation to consider the theological beliefs that describe what faithfulness to God looks like. It builds on the biblical work of the previous chapter. The Bible can be used to support arguments that deny hospitality to those who are perceived to be different. When faced with those arguments, parents need help in examining their own assumptions, knowing what to say to others and what to teach their children.

We all struggle with Jesus' response to the question, what is the greatest commandment? "You must love the Lord your God with your whole heart, with your whole being, and with your whole mind. This is the first and greatest commandment. And the second is like it: You must love your neighbor as you love yourself" (Matt. 22:37–39).

Why do some of us have rigidly bounded tables with limited seating? And why do some of our churches have open tables where all are welcome? What is the role of the church in teaching and learning about living in a world that is diverse in culture, faith, and family formation? In other words, who has a place setting at the table? Whom do we welcome? Whom do we exclude? Why?

I think the answer to these questions can be found in our understanding and practice of the sacraments of baptism and communion. In receiving these gifts of God, we are invited to live in response to them. Having been welcomed with water, we are invited and expected to welcome others. Having been fed at the table where Jesus Christ is the host, we are then invited to sit at table with others and break bread. Perhaps one of the greatest challenges for Christians today is to struggle with a sacramental identity and how we learn to live with that identity in the face of all the difference that surrounds us. This chapter will consider the table God has set before us. At this table it's possible to hear many kinds of music, tell and hear stories from many traditions. The invitation list is an inclusive one!

POURING THE WATER

The liturgy of baptism in most of our churches offers few surprises. Several years ago, I opened up the worship bulletin at my church to scan the liturgy for the day and noticed something I had never seen before in the order of worship for Sunday morning, "Presentation of a Child." My curiosity was immediately piqued. I worship in a large urban congregation that includes the sacrament of infant baptism the second Sunday of every month. This was obviously not a baptism.

The minister walked forward and began with these words: "Every child is a reminder of God's goodness and mercy. Every newborn is a witness to God's marvelous creativity and ongoing creation. Every baby bears the very image of God, and so every birth is an occasion of celebration and profound gratitude." (Buchanan 2006)

The liturgy continued: Her parents have decided that as she "grows to know the God of Abraham and Sarah, Isaac and Rebekah, Jacob and Rachel, she will do so formally through the teachings, rituals, and practices of the Jewish faith. And she will also come to know God, as all of God's children do, through the love and nurture of those around her. We join [this child] and her parents today in celebrating that love of God made known to us, the knowledge that God knows and blesses all of God's children and that she, and we, are all part of the wonderful family of God."

Then questions were asked of the parents and the congregation. "Do you promise to raise your child in our common tradition, imparting to your daughter our shared values, our respect for diversity, our commitment to peace and justice, and our intent to love our neighbors as God as loved us? People of this church: do you promise to support [the child's mother] in her vocation as this child's mother, and do you promise to include [this family] in our concern and prayers for the families of this congregation?"

The liturgy concluded with a prayer for the family. "Gracious God, we give you thanks for this child, and we ask your blessing. Watch over [this child]. Keep her in your care. And we ask your blessing for her parents. Give [these parents] your good gifts of strength and patience and abundant love as they raise and nurture their child. Be with them in the important days ahead and keep them forever in your care. We pray in your Holy Name."

I thought about this simple yet profound ritual and what it was communicating to the family and the congregation about God, the role of parents as faith educators, the commitments of a community of faith to supporting parents and nurturing children, and how we live together in this religiously diverse world, and in this particular case as Christians and Jews. I wondered if anyone else had picked up on the implications of this simple liturgy of blessing a child.

This was not a baptism, yet this blessing of a child shared the liturgical elements included in a baptism: theological affirmation; statement of intention; questions and promises; and a concluding prayer. It began with a theological statement about God that made these affirmations: We are created in the image of God, who is good and merciful. Our birth bears witness to God's creativity and affirms that God's work as creator is ongoing. This first section concluded with a statement about the response of God's people in thanksgiving to God for God's continuing work as creator.

In the second section, there is a statement of intention, which includes these affirmations: Diversity is a reality in both the culture and the church and is an example of the goodness of God's creation, something to be celebrated. Diversity of faith traditions in the family offers an opportunity for religious education, learning about difference. Raising children with practices of faith is essential for their growth in the life of faith and this is the responsibility both of the family and the congregation. In worship, a congregation makes these affirmations of faith: God loves us; God knows and blesses all God's children; God's family is inclusive, welcoming all people.

The third section included an opportunity for the parents and the congregation to make public promises of their faith commitments. The promises included these affirmations: Jews and Christians share a common tradition and common values of respect for diversity, commitment to working for peace and justice, loving neighbors as God has loved us. Christian congregations live as community caring for one another with actions and prayers.

A prayer of thanksgiving and petition also included a theological statement about the attributes of God, who is described as gracious, caring, strong, patient, loving, one who bestows blessing on the creation, one with an abiding presence, holy.

This brief liturgy is an example of theological issues integral to the discussion of diversity. It was written in response to a request by a church member. Knowing that their daughter's birth would be welcomed in a Baby Naming service at her husband's synagogue, she had contacted her pastor to see if there was a way that shared faith commitments to their daughter could be recognized in worship in her congregation.

I wonder how others who were present that day responded to the explicit statement about religious diversity. I wanted to have an immediate discussion with those around me about what they heard in the liturgy and how their faith experiences prepared them to engage with theological affirmations. I was quite sure that there would a variety of responses to the affirmations about diversity, particularly religious diversity. How one understands the nature and work of God is foundational to a person's belief system.

In writing about a Christian approach to religious diversity, Cynthia Campbell notes distinctive marks of the ways that Christians "do theology." For Christians, faith begins with God, "an orienting perspective" that we share with Judaism and Islam. All three Abrahamic faiths share the belief that humans are created in the image and likeness of God. How we think about God is made clear for Christians through scripture. It is through biblical text, through story, that Christians learn about God and grow in our in our theological assumptions.

Also important for Christians is understanding the context or "social location" in which God is experienced and the Christian life is lived. So in what ways is your understanding about God, your theology, impacted by your cultural location? Who are your conversation partners? In what ways are your questions of faith supported or challenged by others?

Campbell believes that we are enriched by varieties of perspectives about who God is and the ways in which God acts in the world. "While I as an individual or member of a faith community may not share the experience of the one reflecting and writing from a different context, their reflection may well shed light on the truth of God in ways that my own experience obscures or makes less obvious. Taken together, this variety of theological reflection has the potential to lead us all into an understanding of God that no one person or no one tradition can achieve alone." (Campbell 2007, 8)

The theological, biblical, and educational assumptions embedded in the affirmations of the second and third parts of this brief liturgy are essential foundations for those who are committed to formation of children for a life of faith. They are foundational for congregations committed to an invitation to the table that is inclusive, welcoming of families that are diverse in culture, faith tradition, gender, and abilities.

When I read over the liturgy for the "Presentation of a Child," I am struck by the connection between the *Shemah* in Deuteronomy 6:4–11 and the acknowledgement of how this child will learn about her faith both formally through teachings and rituals, and informally through daily practices.

Love the Lord your God with all your heart, all your being, and all your strength. These words that I am commanding you today must be on your mind always. Recite them to your children. Talk about them when you are sitting around your house and when you are out and about, when you are lying down and when you are getting up. Tie them on your hand, as a sign. They should be on your forehead, as a symbol. Write them on your house's doorframes and on your city's gates.

Two parents, two faith traditions, one child. Two parents, two faith traditions, one child, two congregations, one Jewish, one Christian. Both parents love God with all their heart. Both parents are committed to teaching this love and living God's love with their children.

There was no water, no baptism, but rather a blessing. I can imagine that some in the congregation immediately noticed this while others may have silently wondered why we were doing a blessing and not a baptism.

There are three Christian approaches to religious diversity and they could have all been present that day: the child is not Christian, she is not baptized, she is outside the church (exclusivist), or her faith is in God's hands (inclusivist), or her life is enriched by growing up with faithful parents who will help her learn about God from two different faith perspectives, Jewish and Christian (pluralist).

As in a baptism when water is poured, questions were asked of the parents and the congregation. In making their promises they acknowledged and affirmed that Jews and Christians do indeed share a common tradition. It is in the Hebrew Bible that we read and hear stories of creation and family, poetry and wisdom, words of prophets and promises of covenant. It is in that part of our Bibles that we first learn of God's creating work, God's Spirit hovering over the waters of creation, God's ever faithful love for all creation.

These parents, a Jew and a Christian, promised that together they would teach their children the values that are shared in their traditions: *tikkun olam* (repair the world) and stewardship (taking care) of all of God's creation.

They promised that they would teach their children to respect diversity, to work for peace and justice in the world, and what it means to love neighbors. And in turn the congregation that day promised to support this family and to keep them in their prayers.

I wish we in the congregation could have been asked one more question, one that would have held us accountable to the same expectation as these parents. Do you promise to be open to dialogue and experiences with persons from other faith traditions? Do you promise to learn about your own beliefs so that you can be an intelligent conversation partner in interfaith dialogue?

SETTING A TABLE OF FAITH

Have you ever really looked at the tables at which you eat? Next time you are at church, take a close look at the communion table. Sometimes there are words carved in it like "Do this in remembrance of me." A church was getting a new communion table and the minister asked that these words be carved on the side where the minister stands: "Feed my sheep." Sometimes there are communion symbols visible: cup, grapes, bread, wheat. Perhaps your church has banners or table runners (paraments) that are visible on communion Sundays. What words or symbols are visible and how do they help you connect with the meaning and practice of this sacrament?

Now take a look at the table in your home. Some tables are round or square. Some tables can be expanded with leaves. On holidays when the table needs to be enlarged for a gathering of family and friends, we go to the closet and get out the extra leaves to make more room.

There is a connection between these tables we set, the sacramental table at church and the family table at home. How you think about the connection between the tables is an important part of your theological understanding and practice of this sacrament.

When I am presiding at the table in the celebration of the Eucharist I usually like to use the postresurrection story of Jesus when he met the disciples walking on the road to Emmaus for the invitation to the table. The disciples walked with Jesus but had no idea who he was, just a stranger, they thought. "After he took his seat at the table with them, he took the bread, blessed and broke it and gave it to them.

Their eyes were opened and they recognized him, but he disappeared from their sight" (Luke 24:30–31).

There is something about breaking bread together. In the story of Jesus with his disciples, notice his actions of taking, blessing, breaking, and giving bread. These are the same actions that Jesus used at the Passover meal with his disciples in the upper room. Take, bless, break, give, and, in doing this, he asked them to "remember me."

Take, bless, break, and give—not hoard, not keep. In addition to remembering Jesus and his life and teaching, this meal also provides a window into the nature of God. We are invited to a table in the world that God has set before us. It is a broad and wide table and sometimes we only see a small individual place setting. Rather than seeing the possibilities for taking time to break bread with those who are different from us and the blessings that may come, it is more comfortable to keep the table private, safe, and small. God's invitation list is broader than the one we can imagine.

How we understand and interpret the meal matters. It is both individual and personal, communal and ecclesiological. It is about remembering Jesus, God's son, and the life he lived, and the life he gave out of love for all of God's creation.

Elizabeth Newman has written, "The Eucharist does not simply motivate Christians to practice hospitality; rather, it is our participation in God's hospitality, as through this celebration we are enabled to become Eucharistic, extending God's offering and gift to the world." (Newman 2007, 149)

The table of faith that we set for families in our congregations can be exclusive, open only to those who fit our image of family, a mother and a father and their biological child or children. Or we can set an open table that welcomes the diversity of family patterns already present among us. The ones whom we invite to sit down with us in worship and the ones with whom we choose to share a meal are visible practices of ways we learn to live with the diversity in our world.

Jesus was sometimes surprised by those whom he met while drinking and eating. These women and men challenged his Jewish contextual understandings of relationships. And we may also be surprised by the differences that surround us at the table. These moments of sharing meals at the table reveal the richness we can taste of the infinite mysteries of God.

What does it mean to recognize Jesus? I think recognition is closely related to memory. Remember the people with whom he shared a table, water, or food: a Samaritan woman who was thirsty, a despised tax collector, a hungry crowd and one boy with a lunch of fish and bread. Recall the stories Jesus told: about the people we see or don't see who are hungry or thirsty, without clothes or shelter or in prison; the banquet where the invited guests did not show up and the host was told to go out and invite people from the streets; prodigal children. Don't forget the people Jesus met: those who were sick in body, soul, and spirit; people who were different from him: Samaritans and Cannanites; children and their parents; women who had been treated unjustly.

Remember the connection! We remember Jesus, setting a table of faith in our homes when we:

- Say or sing a blessing—and we begin this spiritual practice when a child is an infant. Beginning a meal by saying thank you to God is a simple way of introducing theological language and faith experiences to even the youngest person at the table. This simple ritual at home enables children to grow up with an identity as Christian.

- Encourage and support adults in constructing a Christian identity that is open to religious pluralism. In what ways are parents supported in their own growth in understanding their beliefs so that they can answer the questions asked by their children? Amy-Jill Levine has written, "The point of interfaith conversation is not to convert the person across the table, but it is also not to abdicate one's own theology for the sake of reaching agreement." (Levine 2006, 6)

- Encourage conversation, dialogue, engagement, reflection on the day, events happening far away and close at home—interpretation and connection with faith. In doing this we help children and youth connect their experiences of the day with their faith, and in so doing we become faith interpreters, practical theologians.

- Make room at the table for others to sit and eat with us—neighbors, friends, strangers, family. Struggle with what it means to be fully committed to your own faith tradition and yet open to discussion of and experiences with people who are different from you—in faith, sexual orientation, class, culture, age, ability.

Coming to the table, tasting food that is different, engaging in table conversation with people from different places in the world and places in the lifespan is an opportunity to live into the mystery of God's big plan for the world. In the abundance of food and people, we learn from each other about those things that make us alike and those things that make us different. We bring our memories to the table, sharing stories of our past. We also bring our imaginations for the way the table can be set.

MAKING NEW SPACE AT THE TABLE

In writing about the ways that Christians can respond to religious diversity, Cynthia Campbell affirms that people are seeking ways to live with and understand their neighbors, rather than trying to impose their own religious beliefs on their Buddhist, Muslim, or Jewish neighbors. She writes that many Christians "want to find ways to live together with others in ways that honor both their Christian instincts of extending hospitality to strangers and their American commitments to being 'a nation of immigrants,' one nation made up of people from many cultures. Indeed, Christians often find that engagement with those from other religious traditions has helped them understand aspects of their own faith traditions and practices in new and deeper ways." (Campbell 2007, 4)

The need for attentiveness to the implications of pluralism for religious educators was noted for me in the early 1990s when Martin Marty, noted American church historian, observed that "many who are in Christian education have had little experience of other spiritual menus." (Marty 1993, 23) I was struck by his use of the word "experience" rather than understanding or knowledge about other religions. I realized that beyond a few experiences of Catholic mass and Friday night Shabbat, my menu was incredibly limited.

Marty went on to write that in addition to limited experiences with religious pluralism, "Most American Christians are woefully unprepared to be responsible agents of their faith. They know too little of its story, its teaching, and its moral framework to exemplify and testify to their faith in a pluralist society. And they know too little about how to live in and respond to a pluralistic culture. So they blend into the culture or are overwhelmed by it, or they desert the faith for one or another of the options in it." (Marty 1993, 20)

Marty's words are still valid, I think. Many American Christians do not know how to live with all the diversities that they encounter—regarding religion, sexual orientation, and culture. And for some, rather than deserting the faith, Christianity is used as a defense against the other, the one who is different from me. Racist, homophobic, xenophobic comments or jokes reveal our feelings and attitudes of fear, hatred, and lack of understanding of that with which we have little experience.

One way to address the narrowness of the "spiritual menu" is to consider a definition. For Marty, "The purpose of education is to take people where they are and help them come to a new point. The purpose of Christian education that is sensitive to pluralism is to provide the widest scope and fairest representation of the surrounding world. The eyes and autobiographies of participants are not the only pedagogical tools." (Marty 1993, 22) So in addition to experiences of other religious traditions, the contexts for learning, the curriculum used, and the commitment to learning about America's religious diversity should become a priority for religious education in congregations.

In his book *The Dignity of Difference*, Rabbi Jonathan Sacks acknowledges the ways that faith traditions provide meaning and purpose to believers. "The question is: can they make space for those who are not its adherents, who sing a different song, hear a different music, tell a different story. On that question, the fate of the twenty-first century may turn." (Sacks 2002, 5)

I wonder how well our congregations are preparing people of faith to understand and live with the challenges of diversity in their midst—family, culture, faith traditions?

Are we making space for those whose songs and stories are different from ours? In what ways do we offer support and welcome for interfaith families in our congregations? How do the tables around which we gather in worship reveal our response to God who loves us, God who knows us each by name, God who blesses all God's children?

Whose place card needs to be added? Who is not on the invitation list? Consider these statistics from the children's book *If America Were a Village*. It provides facts about people of the United States based on a village of a hundred people. With regards to religion in that village: "82 say they are Christians; 2 are Buddhists; 1 is Jewish; 1 is Muslim; 4 practice a wide variety of other world religions such as Baha'i, Sikhism, and Taoism; 10 consider themselves non-religious." (Smith 2009, 14)

In light of the diversity that surrounds us, Martin Marty's words become a challenge to all people of faith. We must know enough of our own faith tradition and personal faith story in order to fairly represent it in a pluralist culture. If we do this then we will be better equipped to respond to the challenge of the affirmation in the liturgy for the "Presentation of a Child" described earlier in this chapter. We will be able to promise that we will join with other Christians in affirming that a priority for the work of all of God's people is to identify and make commitments to the common values we share, values deeply imbedded in our faith traditions: respect for diversity, commitment to working for peace and justice, loving neighbors as God has loved us.

In a sermon on the Eucharist, Rev. Deborah Block reminded her congregation of the great Protestant Reformation theologian, John Calvin, who taught that God intended the Supper to inspire us "to love, peace, and concord." "Like a bread of many grains was his analogy, so mixed together that one cannot be distinguished from another;" (Block 2010) "so it is fitting that in the same way we should be joined and bound together by such great agreement of minds that no sort of disagreement or division may intrude." (Calvin 1960, 38).

And then she invited the congregation to consider the meaning of these words: "And if you still might be thinking that all of this is a bit stale, chew on this as we come to the table in our time": (Block 2010, 64)

> None of the (brothers and sisters) can be injured, despised, rejected, abused, or in any way offended by us, without at the same time, injuring, despising, and abusing Christ by the wrongs we do. . . . We cannot disagree with our (brothers and sisters) without at the same time disagreeing with Christ. . . . We cannot love Christ without loving him in the (brothers and sisters). (Calvin 1960, 4.17.38)

IT'S WHAT WE DO

Calvin's image of a loaf of bread with many grains is even more appropriate for the community of faith that gathers around the table for communion today than it was in the sixteenth century. Jesus invites us to a table where all are welcome. As Christians we are fed with bread and cup and we leave the table to feed others, to break bread with others, to offer water to those who are thirsty. And we do this because we remember him. As Calvin reminded Protestants so long ago, we love Christ by loving our sisters and brothers.

Back to those questions from the beginning of this chapter:

1. What happens when we "skate over" the issue of faith? People do this for several reasons. One is by intentional choice, like the mother in the *New York Times* article. Others skate over it because of not knowing what they believe. Perhaps they are not at home with the faith tradition in which they were raised and have not taken the time to find a new faith home.

Others I think unintentionally "skate over" the issue of faith by believing that church and faith are something they need for their child but not for themselves. These are the parents who want their child involved in all the programs and activities that the church has to offer. The problem is the lack of connection between the faith that is taught and modeled by faithful church members and the living of the life of faith at home. How can you answer the sometimes deep and challenging faith questions of a child if you are not at home with faith yourself?

Perhaps if parents like this knew they were not alone, that there were others in the church with faith questions, doubts, and uncertainties, they would realize that church is a place where all are welcome, to come as they are to the table of love, grace, and hope. Skating over the issue of faith in your own life has implications for hearing and understanding the experiences and faith practices represented in the world's religions.

In a recent book, *Religious Illiteracy*, Stephen Prothero begins with a statement of paradox: "Americans are both deeply religious and profoundly ignorant about religion." (Prothero 2007, 1) In teaching religious studies classes at Boston University, he has come to realize that prior to teaching about world religions, it is essential to first develop a shared vocabulary so as to have a basic religious literacy in order for young adults to be able to engage in dialogue with each other. For Prothero, "religious literacy refers to the ability to understand and use in one's day-to-day life the basic building blocks of religious traditions—their key terms, symbols, doctrines, practices, sayings, characters, metaphors and narratives." (Prothero 2007, 11–12)

Often times it is adults who need the education required in order to have a shared vocabulary essential for religious literacy. "A 1954 Gallup poll asked American to name the founder of any religion other than Christianity. Only about a third were able to do so. In a more recent study the overwhelming majority of Americans freely admit that they are not at all familiar with the basic teachings of Islam, Buddhism, or Hinduism. One reason for this may be that most Americans do not know a Muslim, Buddhist, or Hindu." (Prothero 2007, 33) With increasing religious pluralism it becomes even more important for parents to raise children with religious identity.

2. What does it mean to be firmly committed to both your own faith tradition and to interfaith cooperation? Being at home in your own faith tradition, knowing the basics of the Christian faith, having some spiritual practices that nurture your life of faith, participating in the life of a congregation are concrete ways of making a faith commitment and prepare faithful Christians for active participation in interfaith dialogue. Also important is knowing the basic beliefs of your particular faith tradition within Christianity and being able to articulate that to someone else. Interfaith dialogue assumes people are able to represent their faith in the conversation.

Knowledge and experience with interfaith dialogue prepares Christians for active witnessing to their faith. When a group of Muslims wants to build a mosque in your city or even near your neighborhood, how will you respond? Will you join other persons of faith in supporting them? Or will you join Christians who mistakenly believe that all Muslims are terrorists and so seek to prevent them from building a house of worship? Being committed to living in an interfaith community requires much of us. Are you ready?

3. What are we called to question and what are we called to affirm? A former student of mine is now a pastor of a wonderfully diverse congregation in Brooklyn, New York. Their church school is described in the next chapter. The issues they face are both deep and broad. Here is a snapshot of family realities in this congregation that illustrate the challenge of questions they face and affirmations that present themselves.

- We have a new member with a two-and-a-half-year-old boy. She was raised by Hindu parents in Trinidad. In her late teen years she started attending church. Then she moved to London, England. While there, she was an active part of a Pentecostal church, where she helped in the Sunday school, and she knew she wanted to come back to church.

- We have a family in which the mother grew up Roman Catholic. The father, on the other hand, describes his mother as someone wanting to explore faith. He and his siblings had major stops in Reformed Jewish synagogues, Episcopalian churches, and Roman Catholic churches.

- We have a family in which the father grew up in the Greek Orthodox Church and the mother spent some time in our church, but also spent considerable time out of the church.

- We have a family in which the parents were raised as devout Roman Catholics and were sent to Catholic parochial schools. Their children currently attend a Roman Catholic school.

- We have another family from the Evangelical tradition. They have two young children and are actively exploring the differences between the churches and traditions of their childhood and that which their children are experiencing here.

- In our high school classes, the majority of children are present in our church and their parents are not. We have young women who felt called to come to church in their teenage years. They live with their mother, who is Catholic, though not attending church. We have several teenagers whose parents are Muslim. The relationship with their teacher is very solid. Our church will not proselytize their children, and the parents are roughly aware of the curriculum and its goals, but obviously it would be different from their theology. (Aja-Sigmon 2010)

For Rev. David Aja-Sigmon, pastor of this church, this difference of faith within families reveals the kinds of issues and questions that parents bring when they seek a church home for themselves and their family. These snapshots also reveal the hospitality and welcome offered by this congregation when they open their doors.

Rev. Aja-Sigmon is convinced that what is needed now in this congregation is a Parenting and Faith series that would provide opportunities for parents to explore the basics of Christian faith from their perspective of being a parent, participating with their children in this Presbyterian Church in this community. The chance for adults to affirm what it is they believe and how that belief has grown and changed supports them as they seek to parent their children in a life of faith.

In an interview for Speaking of Faith on American Public Radio, children's author Rabbi Sandy Sasso spoke about current spiritual challenges for parents.

> I really see religions as different languages to express our spirituality. And I think it's important to recognize that some languages we speak with comfort and some we don't. We find a home. I mean, it's wonderful that there are so many different expressions of spirituality. It's just that we need to find the home that fits for us. And I always tell people, please explore the place you come from, the place you're born into. See if that is a comfortable fit. Because it many times—most times—is, if we're willing to explore it deeply enough, and not to be discouraged because when we were young we had bad experiences." (Sasso 2006)

Parents are called to question the faith of their childhood, to affirm that growth in the life of faith requires honest commitment and engagement with beliefs, questions, doubts. The waters of baptism that mark us forever for a life of faith are not a momentary family ritual. Rather these baptismal waters surround us, supporting our vocation as Christians.

4. *What does faithfulness to God look like?* In his New Year message in 2001 after the September 11 attacks, Chief Rabbi Jonathan Sacks of the United Hebrew Congregations of the Commonwealth offers an answer.

> I used to think that the greatest command in the Bible was "you shall love your neighbor as yourself." I was wrong. Only in one place does the Bible ask us to love our neighbor. In more than thirty places it commands us to love the stranger. Don't oppress the stranger because you know what it feels like to be a stranger—you were once strangers in the land of

Egypt. It isn't hard to love our neighbours because by and large our neighbors are people like us. What's tough is to love the stranger, the person who isn't like us, who has a different skin colour, or a different faith, or a different background. That's the real challenge. It was in ancient times. It still is today. (Sacks, New Year Message, 2001)

"It's what we do!" It's easy to set a table for faith when children or grandchildren are small. Adults are in charge of the meal, of beginning with a blessing or not, inviting discussion or not, even sitting down to have a meal together or not. As children grow and develop and become teenagers, what happens to the tables of faith we set in our homes?

Where are the practices of hospitality and inclusion evident at our tables? Are treasured rituals of blessings still there? Have they changed as kids have grown? A few years after the story that began this chapter, I was fixing dinner for my teenage nephew and a friend of his. It was just the three of us. When dinner was ready, we sat down. My nephew, looked up and said, "Are we going to say or sing the blessing?" I asked him, "What do you want to do?" And he said, "Sing." I looked at the face of his friend, who was probably amazed that he would do that, and I told her the words, "For health and strength and daily food, we give you thanks, O Lord, amen." And we sang the blessing. It's what we do.

3

BLESSINGS

The word blessing probably evokes different meanings for people. Some would connect the word with the act of saying table grace or a "blessing" at meal time. Others would recall the familiar beginning of the NRSV translation of the Beatitudes in Matthew 5:3–12—"Blessed are the ..."The new Common English Bible translates this as "happy are people ..." And others when hearing the word "blessing" remember a friend who when you ask, "How are you?" always responds with, "I'm blessed."

Blessings are things we count as in the old hymn: "count your many blessings, name them one by one."To count our blessings means to remember that this life we live is indeed a gift of God. I think blessings are both hidden and in plain sight. When you look at life through the eyes of faith, then blessings are part of the deep mystery of God's love and presence, which surrounds us like a comforting quilt of faith.

As we learn how to live in a world and culture that is diverse, filled with different kinds of people, we are offered the opportunity to consider how this difference is a blessing in our lives. Take, for example, difference in terms of those who are differently abled. "Stand if you are able" is now a line that is included in worship bulletins or said by the worship leader. I never really thought about it until I was worshiping beside someone in a wheelchair. If you want to share a hymnbook with someone in a chair, then you need to sit down beside that person.

I was on vacation with my family in the summer. One of our favorite evening activities at the beach is going to get ice cream. We came out of the store and my sister and I noticed a mom and dad with their daughter. It was obvious that the child had some mental disabilities. As we were getting ready to leave, we stopped to speak with them. The parents were working on helping their daughter with social skills. Very patiently they helped her speak to us and engage with us in a limited conversation. They didn't push, they didn't avoid the situation, they didn't hide her, as might have been done years ago. My sister and I both commented on the obvious care and love these parents had for their daughter and the gentle ways they were helping her learn how to greet people. And I think silently we both acknowledged this as a moment of blessing for us.

Several years ago I was leading an Advent worship service for a friend at a suburban church in Chicago. After worship on this Friday morning, we went downstairs for brunch. I had my plate in my hand ready for my first bite of breakfast when a woman came up and said she had a question. "My son married a Muslim woman. Now he's not going to church and my grandchildren are not growing up with a faith tradition. My son was baptized and confirmed and now he is not active in a church. I am deeply Christian and I am worried about him and my grandchildren. What can I do?" As I listened to her story and her questions, I realized that this religious difference in her family was not being experienced by her as a blessing but rather as a very difficult challenge to her faith and beliefs.

Rachel is a teenager. She is also a teenager with Down syndrome. On Father's Day last year, she ran to greet her grandfather, the pastor, as he was shaking hands at the conclusion of worship. She stayed beside him. That Sunday as people lined up to speak with her grandfather, they got two handshakes and words of greeting, one from Rachel and one from her grandfather. I felt doubly welcomed and blessed that day.

The transition from elementary school to middle school and high school is not always an easy journey for teenagers. Finding friends and making connections with those who have common interests through sports, music, drama, or academic organizations helps kids in their adolescent journey. Mary was a teenager in high school when she began to realize that she was a lesbian. As she experienced the social world of her peers, she knew that she was more attracted to girls than she was to boys. And she lived with this secret, not knowing what to do with it, with whom to talk, or even how to begin to understand it. Where and how would she fit in? Did anyone else feel the same way? Sometimes being different did not feel like a blessing to her.

Now perhaps you are thinking, "These are blessings? They sound more like challenges to me." And you are right! Behind each of these vignettes of life are struggles. They include difficult and hard questions and additional stories that are unknown to me. Behind these stories that I interpret as blessings—the blessing of difference—are the hard realities of hopes and dreams that parents and families have for their children and their grandchildren, their nieces and nephews. No parents want their child to suffer. No parents want their child to feel the pain of exclusion. No family member wants a teenager to be told, "God doesn't love you because you're gay." Parents want their children to be loved and accepted.

Parents and family members who live and experience difference and diversity on a daily basis want to change the world. They want the world to be a place where difference of skin color, shapes of eyes, sexual orientation, and learning abilities are both understood and welcomed. Families that live with the diversity of faith—Protestant and Jewish, Catholic and Jewish, Christian and Muslim—want help and support for the choices they are making about raising children in faith. And all families dream of a world and indeed work for a world that will see their child and their family not as different or a problem but as a blessing.

Nancy Ammerman suggests that building a religious tradition means "experiencing and telling stories of faith. . . . As people listen and move and see and smell, they are asked to encounter a reality beyond themselves. . . . Creating and telling stories of faith is at the heart of how congregations provide a heritage their children can take with them." (Ammerman 2006, 49)

In this chapter you will meet both individuals and congregations whose stories are illustrative of the ways that we are living with and responding to the challenges and blessings of difference and diversity in faith communities.

As you read their stories, consider your own experiences and how they are similar to or different from these. Consider your own response to these questions:

1. How is my life blessed by living with diversity?
2. In what ways is living with difference a challenge for me?
3. In what ways is my church a place of welcome for all of God's children? What are the issues of difference that our church still needs to address?
4. What do I need to know, learn, hear, experience so I will better understand how to live with the diversity present in the communities of which I am a part?

DIFFERENT FACES: FAMILIES WHO ADOPT

One of the most visible ways that our congregations are becoming more culturally and ethnically diverse is through the adoption of children. Louis Weeks tells the story of going to preach in a strong church in rural North Carolina. On his first visit there that he was struck by how this church was united in its protection of rural life and their sameness. He returned there some years later and immediately noticed some dramatic changes in the congregation. Cultural diversity had come to this rural congregation through families who had adopted children from South America. Weeks observed that "the same protectiveness that had kept them together in their likeness, now was at work supporting them with their differences."(Weeks 2010)

Congregations that have been monocultural now face the challenges and opportunities represented in the faces of their children. Faces that look different from the majority challenge a congregation to think about unexamined attitudes and experiences of living with diversity, and they provide the opportunity for families and congregations to think theologically about the ways that their church extends hospitality.

Hear the voices of parents and children who have been adopted. As you read their stories, think about the implications for the church and how we live and learn together. What are the common threads in these stories?

"Grace has a sister" was the subject line of the e-mail. After two years of waiting on the adoption list, David and Elizabeth got the news that the daughter they had been waiting to adopt from China was ready for them. They had adopted their first daughter Grace four years earlier and she was very excited about meeting her sister for the first time. Grace called her sister the *nihao* baby, *nihao* being the Chinese word for hello.

A few weeks after they returned home, there was a wonderful welcome party for friends to meet Kate. And then Kate was welcomed into the family of faith at her baptism. Behind the wonderful celebrations of welcome to the newest member of this family and to the church family, David and Elizabeth's journey through this adoption process was not without many challenges and some anguish. During their ten-day trip to China to adopt their daughter, David kept a photo journal going through a website so their friends could keep up with every aspect of the adoption process. Their friends in Chicago loved seeing the pictures of Grace and her new sister, Kate, and pictures of Elizabeth holding her new daughter.

Later we learned a bit more about what was going on behind the scenes of these wonderful family pictures. International adoptions are not without challenges for the parents—language, travel, legal negotiations. Also parents must prepare themselves emotionally for what is about to happen. David and Elizabeth were not prepared to meet Kate as they did. She weighed much less than they expected she would for a child who was ten months old. They found out that she had been ill and was still not well and was in need of medication.

They also were not prepared to learn about her abandonment site, information that had not been shared with them when they adopted their first daughter. They learned about this at the moment when the adoption papers were signed and were offered the chance to visit with other parents whose children came from the same adoption home. When David read the papers about their daughter he found out she had been named Guan Qiuyin and was born on September 27, 2005. She had been found as an abandoned infant by the side of garbage pit on the day of her birth.

In his journal, David wrote: "After signing all the paperwork, I walked over and tried to tell Elizabeth what I'd just read. Looking at Elizabeth holding a smiling Kate, I could barely get the words out. Needless to say, we both had to grab hold to get through the rest of the adoption process." (Crawford 2007)

On a visit to the adoption home where Kate was taken and had lived, David and Elizabeth were able to meet their daughter's caretaker. Kate recognized her and it was obvious to them that she had been loved and well cared for by this woman. After a visit with the doctor, they left to visit the site where Kate had been found. Holding her safe in their arms, they recognized and felt the fragility of life.

David wrote: "Of course, we'll never know, but someone in that neighborhood, on that street, saved our daughter's life one day last September. As much as we try to fathom how someone could possibly leave a newborn baby in this filth, knowing, perhaps wishing, that the child would not survive, we know that this child was saved. And we pray for that woman, we pray we can all find forgiveness, and we give thanks for this little miracle smiling in her Snuggly on Elizabeth's lap."(Crawford 2007)

Lynn Turnage describes herself as a single mother by choice. She has adopted two daughters from China. Language is very important in speaking about these adoptions. "Catherine was available for adoption because her birth parents made an adoption plan for her. I tell her that her birth parents knew they would not be her forever-parents.

I also tell her that she was conceived in my heart and soul and being and I had been waiting for her all my life." (Turnage 2010)

Lynn is also very clear about two things. One is that she has her story about her daughters' adoptions and her daughters have their story. Each chooses what they want to tell of their story. Lynn knows that it is her job to protect and support and encourage her daughters when it is needed. She knows when she needs to intervene with another kid or a parent when it is obvious that questions or comments are either inappropriate or harmful, questions like, "Who's your real Mommy?"

Frank Yamada and his three sisters were all adopted by his parents. They did not share much about their role as adoptive parents, "because I think all of us were clear that mom and dad (my adopted parents) were our parents." Frank recalls the story of their adoption and remembers that in the story he heard it was clear that "both the adopted parents and the biological mother (usually the father was not part of the story), loved us and were deeply committed to giving us the opportunities that we should have. As a child, I do not remember having questions about my birth. I think that I never had questions about my birth as a child, because I would have never known to ask. My actual birth was not a huge part of my 'life story.' My adoption was. It wasn't until I was an adult and I had my own children that I began to see the significance of the actual birth process and the ways that our birth shapes the way that we feel received in the world or not. For my children, their actual birth stories are a significant piece of their personal narratives." (Yamada 2010)

Deborah Kapp remembers her children's favorite bedtime story ritual. After reading a book with their mom and dad, the boys had the same request: "Tell me how you got me." They wanted to hear again the story of how they came into their family. And so their dad would tell them one more time, "We saw this baby and we picked him up and gave him a big hug and looked at each other and said, he's ours and he's so beautiful." Children like to hear stories about the beginnings of their life and their family. As Kapp has noted, some adopted children experience the loss of birth stories and a birth family, so telling children their adoption stories becomes a way of helping them claim their place in their family. (Kapp 2010)

She also remembers the deep bias in the culture for birth families. "People spoke about 'real families' as opposed to adoptive families. I knew we were seen as second class when people would ask, 'How can it be a cohesive family unit? It's not your flesh and blood.'" Deborah and Tony adopted two boys, one from Chicago, who is of Laotian heritage, and the other from Korea. She remembers people asking her children, "Where are you really from?"

One way that she dealt with her own identity as the mother of her firstborn adopted son was to count months. "I remember making multiples of nine because that was the length of time he had been nurtured by his birth mother. And when he was nine months, I knew I had nurtured him as long as she had. And then I thought about that again at nine months, nine years." For this adoptive mother, the simple act of counting was a way that she could claim her space in his life, reminding herself that she was just as much a mother as his birth mother, maybe even more.

These stories share common threads that have important implications for us in the church. Adoption stories need to be told and heard from the perspective of both the child and of the parents and other family members. Parents who adopt are stronger when supported and surrounded by a community of faith and love. Churches are an important place for educating about difference in families. What makes a parent a parent? Is it birthing or conceiving someone? Or is it seeking and finding a child through adoption. Surely it is both.

There is another common thread weaving together these stories. God's spirit moves in and among us. God adopts each one of us and make us God's own. God chooses to make us God's heirs. And God's spirit is visibly present in the unknown hands that found, welcomed, named, and loved these children and offered them to parents who had waited for them. God is love—no exceptions, no yes but ...! And the church is called to represent that love to the world.

DIFFERENT FAITH TRADITIONS/BELIEFS: MULTIFAITH FAMILIES

Another way that difference and diversity is experienced in the church today is in the growing number of interfaith families. Families that share two faith traditions also present opportunities for the communities of faith that surround them.

Jan and Joe Feldman are raising their children in a Jewish and Christian home. It is important to them that faith and culture are not minimized. They made the decision to raise their children in Jan's Christian faith tradition. Joe is an active participant in the life of two congregations, his own synagogue and the congregation where his family are members. In speaking about their decision to live as a interfaith family, Jan says that it is made easier when extended family members support the decision. Support not only implies understanding and accepting religious difference, it also presents the opportunity for learning about the faith tradition of a beloved family member.

Regan and Marc Sonnabend met in Jackson, Mississippi, where both were working. Marc is Jewish and Regan is Christian, raised in a Presbyterian church. As their relationship evolved they knew that it was essential to discuss their religious differences and to make decisions before they got married about how they would continue in their faith traditions. They remember saying to each other, "If we're going to do this, let's do it right." (Sonnabend 2010) They believe that having the dialogue about faith and religious traditions has made them a stronger couple. "We love God. We also love God in different ways."

Their experience of family support has been challenging. When Marc's father asked Regan shortly before their wedding if her mother knew she was going to convert, she had to collect her thoughts for a few moments before explaining she would not be converting. He had assumed, likely because of her involvement in Jewish holidays and traditions along with a little wishful thinking, that Regan would be converting.

Regan had wise and patient help from her pastor, who listened to her questions and helped her explore ways that she could live as a faithful Christian in a interfaith marriage. It has been hard on some of her family members, whose beliefs about God are not as inclusive as those of Marc and Regan. Yet when Marc's father died, they came to the service. This young couple are wise enough to know that families react because they care and love them.

While Regan is active in her church, as a family they participate in activities at their congregation, Temple Sholom in Chicago. Rabbi Shoshanah Conover has begun parenting support groups for interfaith families, of which there are a growing number in this Reform congregation. *Havarah* (the Hebrew word for fellowship) or friend circles are offered for interfaith couples raising Jewish preschool children. Meeting in homes and sharing a meal, they have time to hear each other's experiences, share ideas, and support each other in this interfaith experience. Rabbi Conover recognizes the challenges faced by these families and encourages them to include extended family members in life-cycle events such as *bris*, baby naming, bar/bat mitzvah, and weddings.

Kathryn McCabe and Ira Pilchen are another interfaith couple who have made different faith decisions. They are blessed not only with the opportunity to learn about each other's faith, Christian and Jewish, but also with the chance to become familiar with the culture of China, their adopted daughter, Laura's, birth country.

When speaking about the challenges they face as both an interfaith and multicultural family, they comment that there is no magic formula for how it works. Essential for them has been surrounding themselves with other people who have made it work. They speak about the intentionality of their decision to marry, to adopt a daughter from China, to raise her in the Christian faith, and also provide opportunities for her to learn about Judaism. "We think a lot about why we are together." (McCabe 2010)

Like other parents who have adopted children from China, Kathryn and Ira believe it is important for their daughter to learn Chinese and to know about her culture. For the celebration of Chinese New Year in late January or early February, Kathryn sets up a small altar, a Chinese tradition for remembering ancestors. Here she places objects that connect to the traditions of all three family members: a spice box from Ira's family (used at the close of Shabbat), plates handed down from Kathryn's family, and oranges and flowers, which are traditional in Chinese culture.

Shopping at a Chinese grocery store has expanded their awareness of food and culture as has the opportunities they have had to meet other adoptive families. Kathryn and Ira are convinced that parents who adopt children from cultures different from their own have to be open to change, to learning about their child and the culture. Parents must embrace the fact that they and their children will always "share differences" with each other.

Ira and Kathryn understand and acknowledge that they are a different family. This difference is never stated as a problem, rather a chance to learn and grow together. The important support for their "different family" comes not only from their family and friends but also from their church, Fourth Presbyterian in Chicago, where they have found a spiritual home that welcomes them.

These stories highlight the variety of ways that interfaith families make choices about faith and their family:

- Some make decisions early in their relationship about religious identity. This is the case for the families whose stories are included here. Jan and Joe have been active parents in supporting their children's participation in the Christian church and their confirmation. While Kathryn and Ira's daughter was baptized and attends Sunday school, she also participates in Jewish observances at home and with friends and extended family. After their birth, Regan and Marc's children were welcomed with a blessing in both congregations, Christian and Jewish. Now as preschoolers, they are actively involved in Tot Shabbat activities at the family's neighborhood synagogue. These families are making the commitment to journey with their children in the formation of their religious identity as Jews and Christians.

- Some make no decision until children are adopted or born into the family. Then they choose to raise their children in one or other of the faith traditions in the family. Sometimes this works out for families but sometimes the challenge becomes too great. The responsibility for faith formation by one parent requires great commitment and is not easy. The same issue is faced in families where one parent is an active member of a congregation and the other does not attend or participate.

- Some decide to let decisions about religious identity be chosen by the child at an appropriate age—such as confirmation or bar/bat mitzvah. This assumes that a child has been raised in both faith traditions, with experiences of worship or participation in holy days or observances. It assumes that parents have been faithful and patient faith educators with their children so they have grown up learning about what it means to be Christian or Jewish or Muslim or Buddhist or . . .

- Some decide to have no religious affiliation. For some parents the decision to raise their children in the life of faith is made either consciously or unconsciously. This decision has implications both for the family and the extended family. "What will happen to my grandchildren who are growing up with no faith tradition? What can I do?" This is represented in the story about the grandmother that was included at the beginning of this chapter. "I am deeply Christian," the woman said to me. She was obviously worried about her son and his family. I think there were several questions she was afraid to ask out loud, questions such as: What will happen to him as a believer? I raised him in the Christian faith. I did everything right. Now it's all wrong—why? What will happen to my grandchildren who are growing up with no faith tradition? What can I do? This faithful Christian woman is living with some very hard questions.

These families know on a daily basis the challenges of living as an interfaith family. Yet they also believe that the witness of their lives is important. When asked about what she believes is most important to pass on to her daughters, Regan said this.

The values that are such an integral part of our family are to look outside of our biological family for what has become our Chicago family and to share our daily lives with them. We also find it so critical to embrace diversity and to welcome the stranger, which is a common theme in the Judeo-Christian tradition. We already see the girls embracing charity and helping others, which is so rewarding. It seems to me that so much of what is unfortunate about our society at large today can be attributed to sins of omission, not sins of commission. Today was "Mitzvah day" at Temple Sholom. It takes place a couple of times a year. We delivered food from our restaurant, Roly Poly, and saw folks donating blood, giving hair to Locks for Love, and donating old clothes and household items to The Ark.

We have found that celebrating our faith in our home and with our faith communities is such an enriching and definitive experience for us as a family. The theme that I notice over mine and Marc's entire relationship is that when we give of ourselves, we always get so much more back than we gave. That is what I want the girls to carry forward in life with them. It seems that so much that is doctrinal ultimately goes back to "Do unto others as you would have them do unto you." (Sonnabend 2010)

The growing number of interfaith families in our culture presents the church with the chance both to learn with them and to support them in their lives of faith. It also offers the chance for pastoral support of extended family members. How we as individuals and a church respond to these opportunities reveals something of our own faith and beliefs about the nature and power of God's love.

DIFFERENT KINDS OF FAMILIES

I am writing this book in 2010. I remember writing the introduction to an earlier book, *Making a Home for Faith: Nurturing the Spiritual Life of Your Children*. I was talking about the important role that parents have in being faith educators with their children. My friend, Deborah Mullen, invited me to lunch with her and the young daughter of good friends, who were two moms who had adopted a child and were living together as a biracial family.

It was 1999 and I knew I had to say something in the introduction about the different ways that families were being formed and how families look different than they did in 1975. "Parents may be a mother and a father, a single parent, two partners of the same sex, or other family members such as grandparents. Children in a family may be biological and/or adopted. And families may be blended because of divorce or other family circumstances." (Caldwell 2000, 2007, xii) How far have we come as a culture in eleven years? There is still a haunting norm in the culture about what is a family—and a family is for many a mother and a father and children who are born to them. There is more work for us to do as a community of God's faithful people!

Ben and Brad are the proud parents of twins, a daughter and a son. Their children call one of their fathers Papa and the other Daddy. When seeking a church home, it was essential that they find a place where their family would be welcomed and supported. A friend told them about a congregation where they have to come to feel at home.

They began to visit Second Presbyterian Church in Nashville. Each week the worship bulletin of this congregation includes these sentences: Second Presbyterian welcomes you to join us in our journey of faith, regardless of age, race, gender, sexual orientation, economic or family status, ethnic background, or mental or physical abilities. Because words shape our thinking, we strive to use inclusive language in the life and worship of this church. (Second Presbyterian Church 2010)

Ben and Brad talked with me about how it was important to them to find a church home that was open to theological diversity. Like many families in the church, they come from different faith traditions. Brad grew up in a small United Methodist church and Ben was a very active member of a Unitarian Universalist congregation. In seeking a place where they could be at home with their faith, denomination wasn't as important as the culture of acceptance—a place where their theological questions could be asked, a place where they could be welcomed as a family.

"We're a family that happens to be gay" is the way they describe themselves. "We don't put people down because they have different beliefs than we do. We think it's important in a church to create room—for people to have lots of ideas about God." (Bullock 2010)

After visiting Second Presbyterian for a year, they decided to join the church and have their children baptized. When they met with the officers of the church, Brad remembers being very honest with them. "I'm on a journey. I'm not sure of everything I believe. Is there room for me here? I have to be honest about my beliefs and my doubts. I'm willing to cast my lot with you. If you won't allow me to join because of my questions of faith, then it's okay, I'll keep coming here." Brad and Ben were welcomed into membership and their children were baptized on Easter Sunday, 2007.

"We understand we are different. The truth is, we need our children to be protected." They know they are different when another child tells their daughter she is an orphan because she doesn't have a mommy. Fortunately, this family is being supported not just by their church family but by wise and caring teachers and administrators in their children's school. Brad and Ben have a strong network of friends both within and outside the church. Once a month they participate in a dinner group with other adults from the church. Within the love and care of the church and their networks of friends, they are not different.

If the culture that surrounds them in the community and the schools reinforces their difference, then the role of the church becomes even more important in reminding them that in God's eyes, "all are welcome."

Katie, Shelley, Kienan, and Tracy are young adults who grew up in Christian homes and were active in the church. Somewhere along the way in their adolescent development, they realized they were gay or lesbian. Coming out to themselves was the first step in accepting their sexuality, which they knew made them different from their friends at school and at church and different from other family members.

Kienan realized he was gay when he was a sophomore in high school but didn't feel comfortable telling anyone until he entered college. He describes the process as a time when "everything began to start making sense" but he also remembers being terrified and not wanting anyone to know this. "I didn't feel comfortable with it myself, so I just assumed that nobody else would be comfortable with it. How could something you don't like (originally) be able to be liked by those around you?"(Finley, Kienan 2010)

Kienan is fortunate to have parents who know and love him. His mother believes that one thing that is important for parents is to realize that "we cannot out our kids before they are ready, but if we are in tune to them we can help them through this discovery by letting them know that we love them unconditionally—and we do this not just in words but by in our modeling and openness to differences." (Finley, Kristie 2010)

Kienan is also fortunate in being part of a church that loves and welcomes him. At a time when he was not always comfortable with himself and his growing awareness of his sexual identity, he was able to affirm that "there was always a place for me in church and on our youth group and mission trips. No matter what, it felt like a comfortable place for me to be." (Finley, Kienan 2010)

Kienan believes that there is a simple thing that parents can do, "To love who you are and to love the children you have. Parenthood is a gift and people should love the children that they have been blessed with, no matter who they end up growing up to be." His mother knows that her son is "not a blessing because he is gay but because through his struggles he has not only become a wonderful young man, but taught me how to care for a child who is so different from me and others, but is still so much like us." (Finley, Kristie 2010)

Sometimes families know they are different from the beginning. Sometimes this difference becomes apparent over time. And sometimes families make a choice. Bob was a regular visitor to the church. He struggled with alcohol addictions and was trying to get his life back together. A church member made a point of connecting with him and sitting with him in worship. One week Bob brought two children with him to worship. They were living with their mother in the same motel where Bob lived. The sisters were young and had experienced more of the harsh realities of homelessness and drug addiction than they needed. The TV and Bob were their babysitters. Bob knew the church had welcomed him and he brought these sisters there so they could also know something about a home outside their life at the motel.

The church reached out to these girls with welcome and love. It became apparent that Bob was doing his best for the children in the absence of parental supervision. It was also clear that Bob could not do this on his own because of his own struggles with sobriety. One family, encouraged by their teenage daughter and supported by the church staff and social services in the community, offered to take the sisters in as foster children. Two children who had not known the consistency of love, food, shelter or clothes suddenly were surrounded by a faithful family and a congregation.

Three years later, the girls are thriving. They are in the hands of a good therapist who helps them deal with the trauma of their early life. They are loved by a congregation who has watched them grow from fearfulness to trust. They are proud of their new name, the name of their adoptive parents. On Sundays they sit in a row with their foster parents and their adoptive parents. Both sets of parents are quick to say they could not have done this without the support of their church because, they say, "it takes a village" to raise a child.

The realities of the different ways that families are formed challenges congregations to live out their sacramental theology. Congregations who want to recognize the baptism of all people and welcome them to the table where Jesus Christ is the host also need to make commitments to support them with inclusive acts of hospitality.

DIFFERENCE WITHIN FAMILIES

Eight fourth and fifth graders slowly came into their church school room. They all look like typical kids that age. And then slowly, the teacher becomes aware of the differences that were not apparent at first glance. One quickly finished the art project and was wandering around the room looking for some sticks. It was evident that he had something in mind that he wanted to make and he was determined to get it done at that moment. Some were busy at work on their project and another was having a hard time getting started. The shepherd for this class, the adult who is with them all year as they rotate among five different rooms engaging a biblical story with different intelligences, was able to help the new teacher in the art room with the history of some of the kids.

On any given day in church school, teachers in the church school need to be prepared to welcome and meet the variety of kids who come into their rooms. Some enter having been diagnosed with ADD or ADD/ADHD or one of the autism spectrum disorders. Some may roll in their chair and others may be helped in by a parent. And they are all there in one room with all their differing abilities waiting to learn and grow in their faith.

Next door is the kindergarten class, where a child has a fairly rare disorder, Grieg's syndrome, which impacts his motor skill development and also means he can suffer seizures. This is a big class of ten children with two teachers. Charlie Beasley has a buddy, a high school student, who is there with him every Sunday to help him participate. It's a good match. Christopher, his buddy, is learning a lot about special needs children and what it means to be a teacher. And they all work with each other, all this difference, at the same table.

Vanessa Beasley knew that finding the right church home was a priority for their family when they moved. Charlie would need a buddy to help him when he came to church school. Vanessa knows how important it is to initially share information about Charlie and his needs with church staff.

She had two different experiences with bringing her son to church and inquiring about help for him. In one place the church staff was more concerned with Charlie's not disturbing the other kids than they were in his participation. At the church where they are now members, she walked in with Charlie and was met by the director of Children's Ministries, who said, "Tell me Charlie's story." She knew this would be their church home. Here was a place where Charlie would be welcomed and would be a part of a church family who would welcome his gifts and abilities, a place where his contributions would be acknowledged and where he would not be considered a disturbance to others.

Vanessa met with Charlie's teenage buddy, Christopher, to help him understand about Charlie and the best ways to work with him. When speaking with someone about her son she knows that how she introduces her son is important. She wants his teachers and his buddy to be equipped with what they need to know in order to work with him. Yet she also knows that his abilities will change over time as he grows.

When speaking with Christopher about her son, she asked if he had any questions and he said he had one, "Will he grow out of it?" Vanessa replied that he would not, that the gene he is missing will always be gone, yet the way he lives is both organic and dynamic. He will continue to grow and develop and his family will be there watching and waiting with love and support. Vanessa could see Christopher's eyes and knew that he was taking in a lot of hard information about a kid who would be living with this condition for the rest of his life. Vanessa also has enough experience with Charlie's helpers so she knows the kind of young people to look for and, when she finds them, she has confidence that a relationship will be worked out between them.

Jesus welcomed children with unconditional love. Jesus met people and listened to their story. When hands reached out, Jesus offered healing. When questions were asked, he sometimes told stories so they could figure out the answers.

Sue and Jeff are the parents of a child who has been recently diagnosed with Asperger syndrome, one of the autism spectrum disorders. The realities of their son's diagnosis have dramatically affected their family as they have struggled to understand and respond to his needs. Typically children with Asperger syndrome exhibit difficulties with social interaction and may have some repetitive behaviors. These children usually have IQ scores in the average or above average range. They do well with speech and language but have difficulties with conversation. (Newman 2006, 26) To look someone in the eye and have a conversation is not something a child with Asperger's is able to do easily.

Getting a diagnosis for children with autism spectrum disorders is essential for their progress in school because it then becomes possible to get an IEP (Individual Educational Plan). For Sue and Jeff's son, who is in elementary school, this means his teacher and school administrators are able to plan with his parents for an educational program that will meet his special needs. It means that his classroom can be a place where he can thrive, rather than being a place where his differing abilities are barriers to learning.

When they moved to Nashville, Sue and Jeff were looking for a church home where they would grow spiritually, all of them. With teenagers and an elementary child who could be described as socially quirky, they knew they needed the right place, one that would be accepting of kids who are different. "It is important to us that people are willing to get to know our son. With Asperger's, there are rarely physical signs of difference. So adults see him and have expectations that he will act like a typically developing child. And he's not! We hope people won't think he's a bad kid because he won't look them in the eye." (Sue 2010)

They made their decision about a church home because of their son. There they have been welcomed and have found support both through the care of the pastoral staff, the welcoming nature of the congregation, and a support group for parents with kids who are differently abled. Susan thinks about the confluence of the church, the differently abled, and spirituality. As her young son continues to develop and move into adolescence, she acknowledges that he "is so hard to 'read' and too young for me to have any concept on how the church and spirituality will shape his life; however, I have faith that mine and the church's efforts will produce fruit in his life one day. I consider him and others like him to be 'the least of these.'" (Sue 2010)

Kids, like the ones mentioned here, are on our doorsteps with their families, waiting to be welcomed. Vanessa Beasley, the mother of one of these great kids, believes that "many people in educational setting see folks with disabilities as disruptions or barriers to the 'typical' people getting what they need. I have learned that inclusion can mean that we all benefit from the chance to be around people who learn, look, and perhaps act differently than we do."(Beasley 2010) This is the living example we have as we welcome all children into our family of faith, just as Jesus would do.

A DIFFERENT CONGREGATION

Fourth Avenue Presbyterian Church in Brooklyn, New York, is a church committed to living in the intersection of Christianity and other religions as it is faced within families in their congregation. Their website provides a snapshot of this diversity.

> While historically we are an Arabic church, at present Fourth Avenue Presbyterian Church is a community of people from all around the world united in Christ. We are from Lebanon, India, Scotland, Colombia, Syria, Cuba, Pennsylvania, Palestine, Russia, Egypt, Norway, Puerto Rico, Nigeria, North Carolina, and of course Brooklyn! We range in age from a few weeks to 92 years old. (Fourth Avenue Presbyterian Church 2010)
>
> Located at a crossroads of neighborhoods and directly above the subway, we are an urban church committed to staying as a faith center in the city. In an age when people seem increasingly divided, our call is to be a place where people can come together.
>
> Our door is open. Whether the reason is Bible Study, pastoral care, good food at one of our famous potlucks, or one [of] our programs all are welcome here. We believe deeply in the biblical mandate for hospitality and genuine care of people.
>
> We are always searching for new ways to reach out to the city. Come and get to know us, your brothers and sisters in Christ.

This church has been living the intention of God's big plan for mixing the people of God's creation. As they watched their membership decline and their Sunday school die, the remaining members decided to rebuild and, in 1988, they agreed that the Sunday school would be a major focus for this effort. A small Arabic Christian Church was using their hall for worship on Sunday evenings and so they invited the children to come to the Presbyterian Sunday school. One child liked the Sunday school and asked if she could bring her friend, who was a Palestinian Muslim, and that was the beginning of their growth.

Lisa Johnson was eighteen years old at that time and had never taught Sunday school but decided she would give it a try. Now she is the superintendent of the Sunday school and has written this statement about their program:

> For the past 13 years, our Presbyterian Church's Sunday school has taught children who are Muslim. And Catholic. And Greek Orthodox. And Maronite. And, oh yeah, a few Presbyterians as well. To the students and teachers, it has never seemed strange or odd that we have children of different faiths learning and worshipping together. Simply put, it's just who we are. There's always been a sense of tightness in our group, a sense of peace in our classrooms. We have always felt that God's hand was upon our School, nurturing it and enabling it to grow.
>
> We never seek to change these children's religions or to convert them to Christianity. In my opinion, the most important thing that anyone can have is a strong belief in God—the One God of Judaism, Islam, and Christianity. As our minister says, "Christian, Muslim, Jew—we are all close cousins."
>
> The Sunday School's diversity is its strength. It is what makes the group unique, and allows the children to grow in their understanding of their own religion while learning to be tolerant of others' beliefs. Some of our high school students claim that what keeps them interested is the fact that we do embrace all faiths.

None of us who are a part of this Sunday school doubt that God's hand is upon us, that this School is His creation. How else can you explain how children of all faiths—some of whom don't even live near the church—were brought together? Most adults would probably never have invited a Muslim child to come to a Christian Sunday school; only God would have thought to use an 8-year-old immigrant to carry out His handiwork and begin our Sunday school's journey.

And I now realize that God started preparing me to teach this group from when I was a child. One of my closest friends—whom I met in kindergarten—is Pakistani Muslim. We grew up sharing each other's holidays and having religious discussions as far back as when we were in the 4th grade. That friendship has been instrumental in allowing me to understand aspects of Islam and thus relate to our Muslim students. Looking back I realize that while I was reluctant to teach at 18, I now could never imagine being without these children. They have been a source of profound joy in my life—another part of God's beautiful plan.

Our Sunday school has always emanated tolerance and brotherhood. Regardless of race or religion, these kids—and all humanity—are God's Children, equal in His sight. Although our students come from different ethnicities and are of different faiths, they have two things in common: a love for God in their souls, and a love for each other in their hearts.

Lisa's statement shares some interesting parallels with the liturgy for the Presentation of a Child that was examined earlier in this book. Written as a preface for a document about their Sunday school, it includes important theological, educational, and ecclesiological affirmations. Theologically it affirms both the nearness (immanence) and the mystery (transcendence) of God. God's work as Creator is described as both good and ongoing. Diversity in the world is understood as normative and good. God's sustaining and nurturing presence and God's providential care are evident in the ways God is visible in the lives of children. All children are equal in God's eyes.

This statement also reveals the mission and purpose of the Sunday school. The church supports the Sunday school in its commitment to religious pluralism. The Sunday school sees its primary task not as one of conversion but of religious education of children from diverse religious traditions. This diversity is experienced as a strength. The goal of the Sunday school is to enable the participants both to grow in understanding of their own faith tradition and to learn to accept people whose beliefs and faith tradition are different from their own.

The statement also makes clear the theological foundation of the Sunday school, which is a living witness to their understanding and practice of religious pluralism. Most important is belief in God, the One God of Jews, Muslims, and Christians. Faith traditions share two things in common, love of God and love of each other.

In the *Shema*, Deuteronomy 6:4–9, we are told to love God with everything we have, our hearts, our souls, and all our strength. Jesus quoted this Hebrew scripture when he was asked the question, "What is the greatest commandment?" In addition to loving God, Jesus responded that there was a second great commandment, that we should love our neighbors as ourselves (Matt. 22:36). The words of this faithful Christian Sunday school teacher are a vivid illustration of the living out of the two great commandments.

In a world of increasing diversity, Christians seek help in understanding why and how we should be living with our neighbors. This church is a living example of the opportunities and challenges that people of faith have to grow in their understanding of their differencea. The story of Babel is the Bible's foundation story of cultural diversity, and as such it has a powerful effect on shaping our attitudes and those of our children toward our world.

The medieval mystic Julian of Norwich compared the church to a robin's nest and said that it was "meant to protect the fledgling soul until it is ready to fly." (Janda 1984, 20) Congregations that are intentional about living together, faithfully nurturing and supporting all who come to the table, do provide a protected place. And in their coming together with the difference of families, abilities, and faith, together they form the church as a blessing place. Here there is the possibility that faith can be explored, questioned, and affirmed.

Writing about the possibility of confirmation as blessing for adolescents, Robert Browning and Roy Reed have written that "blessing is anchored in an understanding of the sacramental nature of all of life" that knows no separation between the holy and the daily. "God is at the center of blessing but we are active participants in God's blessing as we become channels of God's Holy Spirit in our daily lives." (Browning 1995, 66)

The story about Bob and the two children he brought to worship could have turned out differently. If the church had not welcomed a homeless/jobless person struggling with alcohol, then these girls might have become as lost as their parents were. For Cathy Hoop, the director of Children's Ministries and the rest of the staff, there was no question about making room for Bob and for the girls. Of course there was room at the table! Of course there was a place for them in church school and worship. And because of their support, a family could reach out and make room in their lives and in their home for two young children.

According to the Gospel of Matthew, two days before his last Passover meal with the disciples Jesus was speaking about the judgment of the nations. He was talking about the response of people to those who are hungry and thirsty, those who have no clothes or are sick, and those who are strangers in a new place or are in prison. And they responded, "'Lord, when did we see you hungry or thirsty or a stranger or naked or sick or in prison and didn't do anything to help you?' Then he'll answer, 'I assure you that when you haven't done it for one of the least of these, you haven't done it for me.'" Blessings are truly God's gift to us. As we live in response to God's presence in our life, God's great gift of abiding love is a blessing to us as God's spirit moves in and through our lives.

There is a contemporary hymn written by Marty Haugen, "All are Welcome." The last two verses offer this challenge to people of faith:

> Let us build a house where love is found in water, wine, and wheat
> A banquet hall on holy ground where peace and justice meet.
> Here the love of God through Jesus is revealed in time and space,
> As we share in Christ the feast that frees us, all are welcome in this place.
>
> Let us build a house where hands will reach beyond the wood and stone,
> To heal and strengthen, serve and teach and live the word they've known.
> Here the outcast and the stranger bear the image of God's face
> Let us bring an end to fear and danger, all are welcome in this place. (Haugen 1994)

When all are welcomed into our places of worship, education, and mission, all are blessed. Consider this contemporary adaptation of the Beatitudes as you reflect on your life of faith and the ways you have been blessed.

Happy are families who welcome a child into their life because they will be fed abundantly.

Happy are parents who foster or adopt children from this country and from countries around the world, because God's world is theirs to enjoy.

Happy are congregations who live with children who are differently abled, because they will be made glad.

Happy are families whose children discover that they are gay or lesbian because they will inherit all the blessings of God's world.

Happy are congregations that welcome and support families with different faith traditions because they will see the face of God in all of its difference.

Happy are people who hear mean and ugly things said to them or their children or are questioned or excluded in their commitments to living with difference because they are filled with the joy of their families and their reward is known now and forever as they are held in God's loving hands.

Happy are people in the church who show kindness, mercy, and hospitality to anyone who walks in their door and eats at their table, because they will also receive mercy and kindness.

TABLE CONVERSATIONS

Sometimes they are loud, sometimes there is quiet, sometimes much laughter, occasionally sadness, in these conversations we have around tables. Those who observe cultural trends have pointed out that fewer and fewer families have or make the time to sit down for family meals. As we are beginning to be changed as a culture by social networking through computers and phones, I think the need for human face-to-face interactions will not diminish but rather will increase.

We also gather around a table at church to break bread and share a cup and remember God's son, Jesus, who taught us how to live with each other. And we move from that table to the tables in our homes, and the dialogue continues. Sharing meals with family and friends whether at tables at home or at church provides the opportunity for conversations about our lives and our experiences and reflection on meaning and values.

Table conversations can be places where questions are asked and where it is possible for the faith that we profess to be integrated into our lives. These tables are places where in a community of family and faith we hold each other accountable to that which we profess, affirm, and believe. They are places where we can be both supported and challenged.

This chapter takes a different form from the others. Here you will find practical suggestions for faithful wrestling with living in a world of difference. Some of these will be appropriate for use at home and others for educational settings in the church. They are grouped into categories that I call practices, those things we do on a daily basis that connect us with God and enable our continuing growth in the life of the Christian faith.

In writing about practices, Dorothy Bass has said that they "address fundamental human needs and conditions through concrete human acts—they have practical purposes: to heal, to shape communities, to discern. Practices are done together and over time. Practices possess standards of excellence. When we come to see some of our ordinary activities as Christian practices, we come to perceive how our daily lives are all tangled up with the things God is doing in the world." (Bass 2010, 6–8)

Notice two words that Bass uses, "ordinary" and "tangled." As we struggle to understand how to live with difference, there are simple and ordinary things we can learn. And as we struggle to live faithfully in the world, we do so knowing that God is actively present with us. From the moment of our first breath, all of us, all of God's creation, are indeed "tangled up" with each other in this world.

Craig Dykstra has said that practices "place people in touch with God's redemptive activity . . . . They are means of grace, the human places in which and through which God's people come to faith and grow to maturity in the life of faith." (Dykstra 1999, 43) So in being involved in practices of faith, we participate in God's active presence in our lives and in the world. We then in a sense become God's eyes, ears, hands, and feet, doing God's work of justice, mercy and kindness.

Here you will have the chance to consider six practices of faith: Inviting, Setting Tables, Blessing and Being Blessed, Table Conversations, Choosing, and Taking Time. Like spiritual practices of prayer or reading the Bible or participating in worship, these practices require time and commitment to learn, to grow, to think in new ways about the realities of living with diversity. They can be experienced in a variety of ways, as individuals, as families, and as a faith community. Icons provide a visual guide to these practices.

 A scallop shell denotes practices for families to try at home. This shell is a symbol of both baptism and the concept of journey or pilgrimage.

 Sun symbolizes the light of God. This symbol marks learning activities for small groups of parents and family members getting together either at church or in homes.

 The beehive is a symbol for the church—where all different kinds of gifts and abilities come together. The learning opportunities described here are appropriate for all ages in the church in educational, worship, or missional settings.

Read over them, get some ideas, let them spark your own creativity as you consider practices of faith that invite you to new conversations at the table.

CHOOSING

A reality of life today is the plethora of choices we face. A few years ago I had to replace a cell phone, and the question I was asked at the store caused me to stop. "What do you want it to do?" Being one who was not quite ready for the next step with a smart phone and slightly overwhelmed by all the choices, I said, "Well, make a phone call." I'm quite sure the much younger sales staff had a great time retelling that story.

We make choices all the time, choosing from the menus placed in front of us. Knowing the wide menu of choices faced by teenagers today, parents often remind them of the importance of making wise choices. I think choosing can be considered a spiritual discipline or a practice of faith.

When you choose to give time or money to your church, you are actively involved in practicing your faith. When you choose to take your kids to church school and worship with them on Sunday or midweek, you are saying that this is more important than the other options available to me in the culture. When you choose to confront racist or homophobic jokes or comments made by others, your faithful response to the loving God of creation who pronounced it all "good" is clearly in evidence.

 ### Choose the Books You Read with Your Children

Though many adults now read and listen to books electronically, there is nothing more important than sitting with a child and a book and reading together. The quality and range of books available for children on the topic of this book continues to grow. In chapter 5 you will find suggestions for books to read with children. They are listed in these categories: Family, Bible Stories, World Religions, Diversity (Ethnicity, Culture, Race), Faith/Belief.

- Go online and check out one or more of the titles.
- Give book suggestions to family members who want ideas for birthday, baptism, or Christmas gifts for your child.
- When you find books you like, pass on the titles to your pastor or church educator so the books can be bought for a children's library. Books can also be placed on a book rack outside the sanctuary so kids can select a book to take with them into worship.

 ### Choose to Be Involved in Giving/Sharing with Others

In an article in the online *Journal of Childhood and Religion,* David Jensen writes about his son Finn, who is four years old. Finn goes to a preschool that has chapel twice a week. At the beginning of worship, the children bring their offerings of food that are collected for a food bank in Austin, Texas. Finn calls this "chapel food." David writes:

> He first told me that it's "food that God eats." Now he tells me that it's food that other people eat. Finn lets me know if his "chapel food" is running low. He tells me, "Dad, it's time to get my chapel food," and I've noticed how he gets a sparkle in his eye whenever we bring cans of beans and bags of pasta to his school. He tells me that we need to bring this food so that oth-

ers can eat. What's fascinating to me is how Finn experiences giving not primarily as an act of sacrifice or of giving up something. He'll grow into this attitude, I'm sure. But right now, Finn experiences the act of giving as a joy; and in seeing him give, I have caught some of that attitude as well." (Jensen 2010)

What are some ways that your family can be involved in a project that involves working together, sharing your time and energy in giving to someone else? What options are available through your church or your community? Selecting something together or researching a project could be a family activity with older children or youth. You could follow the Christian calendar and select a different project for Advent, Lent, the season of Easter, and and the season of Pentecost.

 ### Choose to Taste Something Different

The world has come to our communities. We can go to our grocery stores and find so many different kinds of bread: pita and sliced white, tortillas and rice cakes, naan, bagels, and injera, chapatti and cornbread, matzah and croissants, gluten-free and multigrain, and loaves that are fat and round or long and skinny. Behind all these different kinds of bread are stories about culture and class, baking and sharing food.

I have learned a great deal about cultural differences by serving communion and asking people to bring bread that is common at their table. I remember the first time I saw naan or rice cakes and wondered what they would taste like. I immediately went to my computer to look up recipes and information about them.

One simple way to introduce children to the all the variety present in God's creation is through tasting food. If you eat out at a Chinese or Thai restaurant, children learn how to eat with chopsticks. If you go to an Ethiopian restaurant, what fun to eat with the best thing of all, your hands, while you use injera for soaking up the wonderful juices.

Start a family tradition of cooking together on a weekend night once a month. You could choose a recipe from a different country or culture each month. Kids who are old enough to use computers could look up information about the food and the people. This could be an opportunity not only to taste food from a different place in the world but also to learn about another culture. An excellent resource for this is *The Children's Mission Yearbook*, available from the Presbyterian Church (U.S.A.).

 Choose to Be WISE—A Workshop for Families about Difference.
A reality of pastoral ministry today is the need for attention to and care for families who live with the reality of difference. This includes families who adopt children from other cultures, families who are raising children who are differently abled (autism spectrum disorders, Down syndrome), interfaith families, and families who are raising children as committed partners. You were introduced to some of these families earlier in this book.

The reality of their lives is that not only are they working on being good parents and raising children in the life of the Christian faith, they also have to educate others. They and their children have to face the sometimes awkward, insensitive, and sometimes ignorant questions asked by others. Many churches are responding in very helpful ways by offering support groups for parents who adopt children from other cultures or parents of kids with any mental or physical challenges. In these safe places, parents find help and support for each other as they raise their children in a culture that is not always understanding or supportive of their children.

But all of us need education about difference. Consider offering a four-week class on ways to be wise about difference. The class could be offered for all interested adults in either an hour format for church school or a meal and class (one and a half to two hours) on a Sunday evening or week night.

Four sessions could focus on these topics:

Session One—Introduction to the Topic, Overview: How difference takes form in our congregation, identification of questions from participants. Stories shared in earlier chapters in this book could be used as case studies for this first session.

Session Two—Realities of Kids and Families: Have a panel of parents representing some of the diversities in the church talk about some of the situations they have faced with their child(ren), what they need from their church, what they and their family have to offer to the church.

Session Three—Resources for Ministry: books, websites, sharing of practical information. The Center for Adoption Support and Education is an independent nonprofit adoptive family support center. They have developed a great program called WISE Up. WISE is an acronym for four ways adopted kids can respond to anyone who asks them questions about their adoption, questions like: Why are you adopted? Or Who or where is your real mother or father? Kids can choose to be wise when they:

- Choose to **W**alk away from a question, to not respond.
- Choose to respond by saying "**I**t's private."
- Choose to **S**hare something about their adoption story.
- Choose to **E**ducate others about adoption, correcting incorrect information and thus making people wiser. (Schoettle 2000)

Although designed as a program for adopted kids, WISE Up also works for other kids who may be singled out by others as different.

Session Four—Response of the Congregation. practical discussion of ways the church can help nurture and support these kids and families; discuss implications for Christian education and teaching and learning with these kids.

 Choose to Learn about Other Faith Traditions

The chance to learn about another religion can sometimes present itself to you daily as you work with a colleague whose religion is different from your own. Sometimes the news in your city of a Muslim community wanting to build a Mosque where they can worship and educate their children brings out vocal opposition from well-meaning Christians whose understanding and knowledge is limited, incorrect, or driven by fear. And you wonder, "What do I need to learn about the faith tradition of others so that I can be an intelligent and informed world citizen? What do I need to know so that I can help my children or grandchildren learn about living as a Christian in a religiously pluralistic culture?"

One way to help with these questions is to provide a class or conversation group for adults or youth and adults about world religions. It could be offered in varieties of settings: Sunday morning, Sunday evening, midweek. A title such as "World Religions 101—What We Share, How We Differ" could offer learners the opportunity to become familiar with the basic questions and answers offered by some of the major religions of the world. The length of the class would depend upon how many religions are discussed. Consider including these: Judaism, Islam, Hinduism, Buddhism, Confucianism.

Topics for discussion/presentation could be organized around some of the following questions. Books and resources that could be used for this class are listed in chapter 5.

- Bring to class your "Big Questions." What do you most want to know about one of the religions we are going to study?

- In what ways are the world's religions alike? Different?

- What holidays and holy days do various religions celebrate?

- It has been said that the religions of the world converge on the topic of ethics but that they diverge over doctrine, ritual, mythology, experience, and law. (Prothero 2010, 3) Do you agree? Why or why not?

 ### Choose to Know Your Own Faith Tradition

Plan intergenerational/church family events. A way to support the growth in the life of Christian faith of adults and kids is to offer a series of intergenerational events that focus on important seasons of the church year. These events could be planned cooperatively by or in conjunction with several church ministry groups or committees, such as Christian Education/Nurture, Worship and Mission/Service.

Be attentive to how you include the variety of kinds of families in your congregation.

Advent Workshop. A church family event with dinner and a variety of activities for all ages: Make an Advent wreath, make an Advent calendar or paper chain, help decorate the church, make Christmas cards, share Advent stories (invite everyone to bring a nativity/crèche). An excellent resource for this is Martha Bettis Gee, *Things to Make and Do for Advent* (Louisville: Bridge Resources, 1997).

Christmas Eve Family Worship. Consider offering a forty-five-minute Christmas Eve family worship designed for parents with young children and parents with special need kids. The sermon could be a simple reading and projecting of pictures from a children's book that tells the Christmas story.

Beginning Lent. Ash Wednesday is often observed with worship and the receiving of ashes to remind us of repentance and to mark the beginning of Lent. Another way to begin this season would be to offer a simple soup and bread meal prior to the Ash Wednesday worship service. Help parents think about ways they can observe some Lenten spiritual practices with their children by providing handouts or bookmarks with suggestions for individuals and families. On one side provide suggestions for practices they can "Take Up" and on the other side practices they can "Give Up."

A Walk through Holy Week. Often our Holy Week services on Maundy Thursday and Good Friday focus on adults, and sometimes youth. Offer an opportunity for families to come to the church on Holy Saturday to experience a Gospel account of Holy Week by walking through Palm Sunday to Easter. Different rooms could be set up as stations for children and parents to experience the events of Holy Week. Each room could be decorated appropriately to the theme and facilitated by a storyteller dressed in costume.

- Palm Sunday—A storyteller could give a first-person account of watching the procession into Jerusalem.

- Upper Room meal and foot washing—A storyteller would tell about the Passover meal in the upper room and ends with foot washing for each participant.

- Jesus praying in the garden—A storyteller could play the role of one of the disciples who watched Jesus and overheard his prayer in the garden.

- Peter's denial of Jesus—A storyteller as Peter would tell his story.

- The angel and the empty tomb—A storyteller as the angel would greet each one and tell the story of the women coming to the tomb looking for Jesus.

- Easter—Set up the last station in the sanctuary. Here the pastor could meet children and parents and help bring together the five stories of Holy Week. One way to conclude this Walk through Holy Week would be to have a large wooden cross covered with chicken wire. As families leave, they could be invited to help cover the cross with flowers for Easter Sunday.

Pentecost Sharing. We do a good job of celebrating Pentecost, the birthday of the church, in worship. We retell the story of the early Christians and the movement of God's spirit in and among them. God's breath moved in and among these people and they became aware of their difference as all of sudden varieties of languages were being spoken.

Consider expanding the Pentecost experience by planning a variety of options for ways church members of all ages can be involved in service and mission either on Pentecost Sunday or on another day. What if this day of service could connect your congregation with another religious group in your community? I got this idea from seeing the announcement of such a day at a synagogue in Chicago. *Olam Ha Mitzvot* (A Day of Good Deeds) provided a variety of service activities for all ages. Projects included were: a blood drive; collection of clothing, furniture, household items for a social service agency; visiting with residents of a nearby retirement center; knitting and crocheting blankets for the elderly for Warm Up America; young adult work project at a women's center; family activity decorating lunch bags for shelter guests; teenagers and families gardening project; Locks of Love donation opportunity.

All of these activities happened on one day and people signed up for the one in which they wanted to participate. Use this model as an idea for your congregation as an experiential way to celebrate the power of God's spirit moving in and among us, blowing us in ways we can never begin to imagine!

 ### Choose to Examine Racism and Prejudice

This could be one of the hardest choices to make because no one likes to admit they are either racist or prejudiced—"No, not me, never"! In an article for the journal *APCE Advocate*, Adele Halliday writes that the more obvious forms of racism take shape in racial slurs or personal attacks upon a person. Other forms or racism are more deeply embedded and need to be examined.

> Institutional racism manifests itself in the policies, practices, and procedures of institutions, which may promote or sustain different privileges or advantages of some individuals. Cultural racism, embedded in a society's value system, is a network of beliefs and values that justify discrimination, and is maintained through the socialization of individuals through schools, media, and families. Systemic racism involves the rules, regulations, and laws of society, which are woven into the whole societal system and which result in unfair treatment, discrimination, unfair access to jobs, housing, schools, and healthcare. (Halliday 2007)

But we are human, and like the people living in Shinar who wanted to stay together because they liked it that way and decided to build a great tower (Babel), when we fail to examine our own assumptions, attitudes, and uses of power, we can indeed be engaged in racist thinking or acts that harm others. What towers of ignorance, prejudice, or power assumptions are we continuing to build? What towers of exclusions, privilege, and racism? In what ways are we involved in the three kinds of racism described by Halliday?

Consider these suggestions for discussion in your congregation. Settings for these discussions can vary according to the needs of your congregation. These ideas could take form in a church school class, an intergenerational (youth/adult) Sunday night discussion, vacation Bible school, a Lenten house-church conversation, or a retreat.

Study Sessions. Use some or all of the resources from *The Racism Study Pack*, available for $53.00 from www.thethoughtfulchristian.com. In the study pack of eleven sessions are leader's guides and learners' resources for dialogue about the question, Why is it so hard for Christians to talk about race? The study pack provides a tour through the biblical and historical realities of race and racism as a foundation for asking difficult yet necessary questions about where we stand today— and where we must go from here. Study titles include: "Why Is It So Difficult to Talk about Racism?" "Racism 101," "The Bible and Racism" (2 sessions), "A History of Racism in the United States" (four sessions), "White Privilege," "Is Affirmative Action Still Needed?" and "Do Segregated Churches Imply Racism?"

Community Conversation. Plan a conversation about race and racism with other churches in your community. Hearing Our Voices, Experiences of Race, and Privilege and Power might be topics that would encourage persons of color, Caucasians, and mixed-race people to sit together and hear each other's stories. Persons trained in facilitating such conversations can be found in most large communities.

Congregational Practices Review. As a board or session or officers of the church, plan a time for discussion about congregational practices that either support God's plan in Genesis that all creation is good or deny that plan through racist or privileged assumptions and acts. Compare Genesis accounts of the goodness of creation with this statement from Article 1 of the Universal Declaration of Human

Rights. This declaration was adopted by the United Nations General Assembly on December 10, 1948, in Paris. "All human beings are born free and equal in dignity and rights. . . ." (United Nations 1948) The Canadian Ecumenical Anti-Racism Network has excellent resources for this discussion. In writing about our necessary work in healing among the people of the world, they remind us:

> The time to dismantle and eradicate racism is now. It is urgent for us and our churches to acknowledge our complicity with and participation in the perpetuation of racism, slavery, and colonialism, or we are not credible. This acknowledgment is critical because it leads to the necessary acts of apology and confession, of repentance and reconciliation, and of healing and wholeness. All of these elements form part of redress and reparations that are due the victims of racism, past and present. (International Ecumenical Caucus 2001)

Resources for this conversation are described in chapter 5.

Movie Night. Plan a Friday night Dinner and a Movie. Share a pizza, watch a movie and then engage in discussion with questions such as:

- What perspective on racism or homophobia do you see in this movie or film clip?
- Where in the movie did you see examples of white privilege at work?
- What dimensions of America's racialized society are depicted in this film?
- What racially coded language or images did you observe?

  Movie suggestions include the following:

- *The Joy Luck Club*—especially the clip where the daughter takes her non-Asian boyfriend to dinner at her parents house.
- *Sweet Land*—poignant movie that tells the story of land, love, and the American immigrant experience.

- *The Hurricane*—the story of Rubin "Hurricane" Carter, a boxer wrongly imprisoned for murder, and the people who aided in his fight to prove his innocenceGood movie for discussion about racism.

- *Avatar*—good for discussion about perceptions about difference. Indigenous people are aliens who are very connected to the earth and are "spiritual"—but need a white human to save them.

- *Traces of the Trade*—A documentary film describing the journey of Katrina Browne, the filmmaker, in telling the story of her New England ancestors, one of the largest slave-trading families in U.S. history.

- *Chutney Popcorn*—a comedy about family and culture (Indian and New York City) and the challenges of difference.

- *Gran Torino*—story of racism in a neighborhood.

- *Lars and the Real Girl*—a story about a small town and the ways the townspeople respond to a person who is perceived to be different.

- *Praying with Lior*—incredible story of the determination of a boy with Down syndrome and his preparation for his bar mitzvah.

- *Because of Winn Dixie*—wonderful story of a girl who finds a dog and how her life evolves. This movie offers great chances to talk about what is faith, where is church, what is community?

- *Crash*—brings out bigotry and racial stereotypes. A synopsis of this movie says that "people are born with good hearts, but they grow up and learn prejudices." (Lewison n.d.)

- *The Kids are All Right*—movie about two lesbian moms raising their kids.

- *Amazing Grace*—a biographical movie that tells the story of William Wilberforce, a British citizen who worked the end the slave trade in Great Britain in the late eighteenth century.

BLESSING AND BEING BLESSED

We begin meals at our tables at home with blessings, words of thanks spoken or sung. We say thank you to God, a blessing in a more formal and liturgical form when we share in the Lord's Supper at church. And before we leave worship, we receive a blessing from the minister. Sometimes we bless others and sometimes others bless us.

When I first heard it, I remember thinking, that's an interesting response. Usually the people who respond to the question "How are you?" with "I'm blessed" rather than "Fine" or "Good" have a big smile on their face. Although I've never asked anyone why she has chosen that response, my guess is that it allows her to make a brief affirmation of faith. Perhaps in saying it out loud, "I am blessed," the person is reminded of the ways that God is present in his or her life—like the author of Psalm 146, who writes: "Let my whole being praise the LORD! I will praise the Lord with all my life; I will sing praises to my God as long as I live."

Blessings can sneak up on us and surprise us, like the three-year-old at church who looks up at you and reaches out for a hug and tells you he loves you, or the teenager who reminds you to "text me." Think about the ways that living in a world of difference and diversity can be a blessing in your life.

A couple who had raised their daughter in the Christian tradition learned that she had decided to get married to a man who is Jewish. And like the couple described in chapter 3, this couple also decided that their children would be raised as Jews. The parents knew they had a choice, to either welcome this difference into their family or to let it disturb them and cause them to be anxious. They decided that their daughter's choice of a spouse and her decision about the faith tradition of their children would be a blessing in their life. They would continue with their family holiday traditions and also honor the faith decisions of their daughter and her family.

 ## Hearing Our and Our Children's Questions

As I have suggested in an earlier book, *Making a Home for Faith* (Cleveland: United Church Press, 2000), parents are the primary faith educators for children. When kids ask really difficult questions, it's easy to say, "Well, I don't feel able to answer that, it's why I take my child to Sunday school." Common questions that arise in conversations with parents curious about this role include these:

1. What does my child understand about God and in what ways does this evolve and change as she grows and matures? Children grow and change theologically in ways similar to cognitive or physical development. The why and where questions about God asked by a three-year-old are often mysterious. They wonder about where God lives, what God looks like, where heaven is. As they move through cognitive changes, they learn more concretely and then in later childhood and early adolescence are able to think more abstractly. Important to remember is that faith and beliefs are not static; rather, they grow with us.

2. When and how should I begin to nurture my child in the life of faith? In Chicago at the time of elections for public officials, there is the joke about "vote early and often." The nurture of children in a life of faith should happen early and often, beginning with the moment she or he is welcomed into the family by adoption or birth. Parents nurture their child in faith by engaging in practices of faith. As Robert Wuthnow reminds us, spirituality, or a life of faith, becomes real and embedded when we grow up living it. In his research he found that children "assimilated religion more by osmosis than by instruction. . . . The parents, teachers, and clergy who understood this best were the ones who created an environment in which spirituality was fully and deeply embedded. They honored the spirituality of chicken dinners, of gefilte fish, of family Bibles, and of stained-glass windows." (Wuthnow 1999, xxxvii)

3. Does it matter what or if I believe, and in what ways do my beliefs impact my child's faith? Unless you as a parent are willing to wrestle with your own belief system, then the other two questions are pointless. Children learn by watching and listening. They watch

us pray, read the Bible. They know when we respond to others in need. They see it all! In raising children in faith, in reading and telling them stories in the Bible, in helping them connect these stories with acts of faith in the world, our beliefs and faith grow with our children, our grandchildren, our nephews and nieces.

The following questions may be yours or those of your child. Hopefully you have found resources in this book for some of the ways you can begin to think about responses that make sense both for you and your child.

- What does it mean to be Christian in a multifaith world?

- What is a Christian response to other religions?

- I am deeply Christian. I raised my children this way but my grandchildren are being raised in a home that is Muslim and Christian. What do I do when they come for Christmas?

- My grandchildren are being raised Jewish. I so want them to know my Jesus. But I also know they are being raised faithfully. What will happen to them if they don't know my Jesus? I wonder about that.

- How do we help our children learn about different faith traditions, even those within our own family?

- What are we learning from our children about difference?

- What do our children and grandchildren learn from us?

- Is there any guidance in the Bible for how we live together, connecting across the ages, culture, race, and theological traditions?

- What is a faithful reading of the Bible?

- What does the Bible say about living with diversity or difference?

- I love to tell the story, but what story do I tell? And how do I tell it to children and youth?

- How has my reading of the Bible informed my own commitments to living with diversity?

What other questions would you add to this list? If any of these are your questions, know you are not alone, that others share them. It is important to find a place and time with friends or family or in your congregation to struggle with your beliefs and your responses, which will evolve and change over time.

 ### Family Conversations—Being Blessed with Difference; Challenges and Opportunities

Consider offering conversation opportunities for parents or family members. They could be planned using the title Short Subjects, with each one having a different focus on a particular kind of diversity experienced by families today. These classes could help support parents and also address issues and questions of extended family members such as grandparents and aunts and uncles or indeed anyone in the church who is a friend of children.

Differently Abled Kids. Steve Siler is a wonderful musician who has written a song with the title "Whole in the Sight of God." In writing about this music he says that it was "created especially for families who are loving a child with special needs. The project includes the song that I wrote that day and a spoken love letter woven from the affirmations of twenty-five parents who are raising a child with special needs. This journey through words and music is a gift of love and encouragement for anyone whose life is touched by disability." (Siler 2010)

Families with differently abled kids already know their child is "whole in the sight of God." It's also important to them that their congregations know this. Our churches can be places of welcome when we:

- Take time to learn about the needs and learning abilities of differently abled kids—kids with ADD/ADHD, autism spectrum disorders, kids with chronic health issues, kids with Down syndrome.
- Provide opportunities to meet parents of kids who are differently abled (and their child) to learn about ways the church can support their participation in the life, education, and mission of the church. What specific needs does the child have?

- Provide a form for parents to complete that helps church staff become familiar with the child. A great example for such a form can be found in the book by Barbara J. Newman *Helping Kids Include Kids with Disabilities* (Madison, WI: CRC, 2001).

- Provide opportunities for educating teachers and youth leaders about teaching and learning with kids with special needs.

- Educate the congregation about how it can live in response to the baptism of kids with special needs by welcoming them in the life and worship of the congregation.

- Think intentionally about how to help other kids and youth know the ways they can be friends to kids with disabilities.

Families with Gay/Lesbian Children. In the process of interviewing gay/lesbian young adults it became clear that one area that concerned them was their parents. They spoke of the difficulty they faced of coming out to themselves first, knowing that their sexual orientation would not be easily accepted by either the culture or by their families. They knew their parents needed help and support but they were not always able to give it.

An opportunity for conversation in the church would provide space and time for the questions and concerns of family members who love their children yet struggle with their own assumptions and questions. Sometimes it is easier to get to your own story by hearing the story of another. Hear some more of the story of a mother of a son who is gay.

> I think the developmental stages of a child's sexuality need to be understood by parents long before they are in the emotional thick of things. I also feel that as parents we cannot out our kids before they are ready, but if we are in tune to them we can help them through this discovery by letting them know that we love them unconditionally—that is not just in words but by our modeling and openness to differences.
>
> It is hard to prepare when part of it is so out of their con-

trol. If we can educate and build that support for parents from the very beginning, before life hits us in the face, we would be better prepared for all the changes children encounter and bring to the table. The church can provide a safe environment for families, a place where they know their child can be a part of the community in a safe nurturing way, and this needs to start at infancy almost. Adults need to be aware of the changes taking place in all areas of an adolescent's life and to be vigilant in their openness to that. They cannot ever forget and make inappropriate remarks about things or people being gay or queer. A remark that someone might think will make them seem cool or connected to the kids can be devastating to a young person.

Opportunities for adults to explore the needs of adolescent sexual identity development can be very helpful. There needs to be an openness to the unexpected and diverse needs of adolescents before adults come face to face with it—anticipation and reflection along with education.

Do such families hide this or are they open? I think most families hide it due in part to the fact that the child's discovery is often later in the high school experience, and by the time everyone has had a chance to absorb everything the child is almost out of the house and on to college or work and in a different peer group. I think that because most parents have a pretty traditional "dream" of what their child's life will be like, the opportunity to explore how these dreams can be different, but still wonderful beforehand is hard. (Finley, Kristie 2010)

This story can be used as a way into discussion of the experiences of those in the group. The following questions could be used to consider specific ways that congregations can support LGBT kids and teenagers and their families.

- How do we become smart about difference, knowing which questions to ask and not ask?

- What support is needed for families of LBGT kids, youth, and young adults?

- What kind of education do we need to offer to those who teach and work with youth who are LBGT?

- How do we provide safe places for honest dialogue about sexual orientation?

 Blessing Multifaith Families

For churches that have families who share two faith traditions, consider the ways that they can be supported. Here are some ideas that religious leaders and congregations are trying. What else would work in your context?

Gather in Homes. For families that share Jewish and Christian faith traditions, quarterly gatherings in homes with kids is a way to help parents connect with each other, share experiences, and talk about the practical issues of raising children in one faith or the other or raising them in two traditions. Discussion about holidays and books for kids, family faith traditions like Shabbat, or blessings at meals help support these families in their commitments to raise children in the life of faith.

Conversations at Church. Consider offering occasional opportunities for extended family members of multifaith couples to get together for conversation. Just as the couples have worked through their religious choices, so too their parents and extended family may be facing really hard questions and decisions to make.

- What are the best ways that we can support them in their decision?

- If we don't know a lot about the faith tradition of the person our child is marrying, how do we go about learning more about it?

- If we don't agree with their decision about raising children in a faith tradition different from ours, what do we do?

- If we want them to come to be welcome in our home at holidays when we celebrate Christmas and Easter, how do we do that?

- My grandchildren are not being raised Christian. They are not baptized. Will they go to heaven? What will happen to them?

Offering time and space in the church for honest questions and sharing of concerns is a way that the faith community can support grandparents and aunts and uncles in their continuing nurture of their children and grandchildren, nieces and nephews. An excellent resource for these conversations is a book by Dr. Cynthia Campbell, *A Multitude of Blessings, A Christian Approach to Religious Diversity.*

Rituals/Blessings—Learning from Each Other. There are other very practical things that congregations can do to support interfaith families:

- Know what religious diversity is represented in families in the congregation.
- Provide resources for interfaith families that help them learn about holy days and spiritual practices.
- Provide educational opportunities and experiences for the congregation about world religions
- Plan for ways that that worship can be a welcoming place for interfaith families, such as the liturgy for the blessing of a child that

TABLE CONVERSATIONS

Some of us have grown up with the experience of lively, challenging conversations and debates at the dinner table. There we have heard our parent/s discuss events going on in the world and their reactions and responses. And we have been invited into that conversation. At these tables politics, race, economics, religion, faith, the church—everything is "on the table" for discussion and reflection.

And then some of us have grown up with very different tables—perhaps more focused on family issues and experiences of the day. And still some have been raised with no family traditions at meals, little time together, and no conversation.

It is interesting to imagine what the conversation must have been like when Jesus visited in the home of Mary and Martha, or shared a meal with Zaccheus or the disciples. I like to imagine his questions: So what did you notice today about the people we met? What did you hear them say after I invited myself to eat with the tax collector? What was their reaction when I accepted water from that Samaritan woman? And why did you think I would not want to greet the children? So who do you think that I am? And what is the most important thing you are learning from our conversations, from our walks from village to village, from our meals together?

Consider some of the following suggestions for table conversations. What new ideas for your own practice are evoked by these suggestions for tables in your home or tables in your congregation?

 ### Table Rituals for Families

Beginning a ritual at mealtime with younger children helps get the practice started. What you do can change or evolve as children grow older. Some things may change and new things emerge as children move into adolescence. Here are a few suggestions that help connect the table, life, and the life of faith.

Share. Encourage each one around the table to share something from his or her day—"Sads and Glads" or "Thorns and Roses."

Sing or Say a Blessing. There are so many ways to do it. Say a simple blessing together as a family. Or each person takes a turn offering a blessing during the week. Or try one of these prayers. The first four are included in the children's book *A World of Prayers.*

- From China: Each time we can, may we remember God's love.
- From Germany: Come, Lord Jesus, be our guest and let these gifts to us be blessed.
- From Scotland: Doon head, up paws, thank God we've jaws.
- From Nigeria: The bread is warm and fresh, the water cool and clear. Lord of all life, be with us. Lord of all life, be near. (Brooks 2004)
- From Judaism: You are Blessed, O Lord our God, who has kept us alive and sustained us and enabled us to reach this happy time.

Neighbors Near and Far. Keep a map of the world and/or a newspaper nearby or accessible electronically and discuss pertinent questions: What neighbors near and far are we praying for today? Who in our community needs some immediate help? What can we do as a family or a church to respond?

Calendar Check—Keep a calendar on the table. It can be used to help you connect with images and information about faith traditions. A great Christian calendar is "Salt of the Earth, A Christian Seasons Calendar," which begins with Advent each year. It is available from www.christiancalendar.com. Each year the Multifaith Action Society produces a beautiful calendar that is filled with artwork and information about monthly celebrations of the religions of the world. It is available from:www.multifaithaction.org.

Table Talk

Consider offering a three-week class for parents that provides them with the chance to reflect on how they were raised as children. Many of our churches have people attending who were raised in other Christian faith traditions. You also are probably aware of families where one parent is active in the church and the other is not. Sometimes that lack of participation comes from having been burned by religious upbringing as a child. Sometimes it's a factor of belief and doubt. Wellesley Hills Congregational UCC Church in Wellesley Hills, Massachusetts, says it clearly on their website about their welcome to everyone: We welcome all who want to thank God, as well as those who have doubt, or do not believe. We welcome people of all ages and family configurations.

Week One—Growing Up Christian

Focus: Provide overview of the class sessions. A great introduction to this topic is the video, *How Do You Spell God?* In cartoons and interviews, children's questions of faith are depicted. Used copies can be found on the Web. Invite conversation around these questions:

- What are your memories of growing up religious or not?
- What spiritual practices were a part of your home as a child?

Week Two—Holding On, Letting Go

Focus: Honest dialogue about the realities of growing up religious, identification of questions of belief and faith, and discussion about hopes and fears as a parent.

- What questions of faith do you struggle with?
- What do you want to hold on to, and what do you want to let go of regarding your own experiences of growing up religious?
- In what ways are your experiences from your childhood relevant to your own role as parent?
- What is your greatest hope for your own child/children regarding growing in a life of faith? What is your greatest fear?

Week Three—Family Practices of Faith

Focus: Review some of the information shared in this book about practices of faith. Other resources can be found in chapter 5. Provide time for people to identify the practices of faith they would like to try and do in their home with their children.

 ### Moving from the Table and Continuing the Conversation

Second Presbyterian Church in Nashville, Tennessee, works intentionally to help its members connect the table where they share the Eucharist with living in response to eating the bread and drinking the cup given to them in the name of Jesus.

During Lent in 2010, they decided to focus on the corporate sins in which humans participate in as a society. So each week in worship a Minute for Mission in worship featured a brief presentation by a representative from a local agency committed to working for change in the community. After worship, everyone was invited to meet the representative to ask questions or share ideas and to engage in the spiritual practice of speaking truth to power by writing letters of support. Groups from the community who were represented at these tables were: Tennessee Alternatives to the Death Penalty; Living Waters for the World; Not for Sale, a Campaign to Abolish Contemporary Slavery; Bread for the World; Homelessness and Room in the Inn.

SETTING TABLES

In the past few years, I have become a quilter. I love the challenge and creativity involved in making quilts. A friend of mine has been quilting smaller projects like table runners for years and she shares ideas with me for patterns and themes. Leftover pieces of fabric from larger projects can easily be used in the quilted blocks for these runners. A simple table runner helps set the table for food and those who gather around it.

In addition to setting tables around which we gather for nourishment, it is also essential to set a table of faith, to think in intentional ways about how family members are nurtured in the life of faith. How do you set this table? Using the analogy of the quilted table runner, what blocks of faith do you add to a beginning life of faith?

 ### Spiritual Practices at Home

As I listen to parents talk about their desire to do some things at home with faith practices like prayer or reading the Bible, I also hear their confessions of not knowing where, when, or how to begin. Sometimes they also admit that they didn't really grow up doing anything like this and so are clueless about what to do. Others are quick to say they don't want to replicate the practices they grew up with. For families with two faith traditions at home, such as Protestant and Jewish, this is an added challenge and opportunity.

So to make it simple, imagine three ways of engaging in spiritual practices at home. Remember the prophet Micah, who tells God's people that all that the Lord requires of us is to do justice, love kindness, and walk with God. Another way to think about it is Pray, Fast, and Share. Three things common to the three faiths of Abraham and Sarah are prayer, fasting, and sharing. These acts of faith that form us, challenge us, and connect us with those in need are blocks of faith that unite Christians, Jews, and Muslims.

Pray. We can learn to be calm, to be quiet, or even to say a prayer when we are very busy or anxious.

Teach children to pray by saying prayers with them at meal times. Practice different kinds of prayers. In their book *How Do You Spell God?* Marc Gellman and Thomas Hartman describe four kinds of prayers that kids (and adults) can pray: Thanks (thanksgiving), Gimme (intercession, like when we pray to God for others), Wow (adoration and praise to God), and Oops (confession—I made a mistake, please forgive me). (Gellman1995)

- Breath prayers—This is a prayer you can say in one breath: "The Lord is my shepherd." "Thank you for this day." "Give me rest this night."
- Pocket prayers—Life can sometimes get overwhelming for kids as well as adults. We get anxious and wound so tight that it is hard to get out of the anxiety, relax, and breathe. This is especially true for kids with autism spectrum disorders. On small cards or card stock, write down some "pocket prayers" that they keep in their pocket: "Thank you God for . . ." "Dear God, help me." "God, be with me, I'm scared."
- Prayer boxes—Children are attuned to what is going on in the world and in their family. Making a prayer box is a way to help them include people and places in their prayers. Get a small box, either a small cardboard jewelry box or a shaped box (square, circle, heart, star, or shoe) from a craft store. Invite kids to write names of people whom they want to remember in their prayers or places in the world that need their prayers and put them in the box. Each time they go by the box, they can touch it and say a prayer for one of the persons or places named in the prayer box.
- Make a simple table runner with squares of fabric alternated with blank squares. Using fabric markers, write names or places in the world that you are praying for. If you want to connect these run-

ners with the Christian calendar, you could make them out of different colors for the season of Advent (purple or blue), Lent (purple), Easter (white), Pentecost (red), and Common Time/Season after Pentecost (green).

Fast. Fasting is often associated as a Lenten practice and many Christians have experienced it as a time when you give up something you like to eat as a discipline during the forty days before Easter. So fasting is giving up or letting go. It is also something we share with other religions of the world.

Faithful Jews fast for twenty-five hours starting an hour before Yom Kippur begins and ending after nightfall on the day of Yom Kippur. The purpose of Yom Kippur is to bring about reconciliation between people and between individuals and God. During Ramadan, Muslims fast from dawn until sunset each day. Their practices are similar to those of Jews and Christians as they seek forgiveness for sins and pray for guidance in living life as they seek to refrain from evil actions, thus bringing them closer to God.

"O you who believe! Fasting is prescribed for you as it was prescribed for those before you, that you may become God-fearing" (Quran, 2:183).

Which of these practices of fasting or letting go would work for your family of children and/or teenagers?

- When eating a meal together, leave all cell phones on mute or in a basket in another room so meal time won't be interrupted with texting or calls or the temptation to check one more email!

- Give up all evidences of time on Sundays. Let Sunday be Sabbath, kairos (God's time, not chronos). Consider taking off your watch when you go to church, or leave a cell phone locked in the car when you go to church. Try one day of fasting from attention to time and schedules.

- Let go of TV or games for a period of time each week.

- Reduce your carbon footprint—walk or bike together at least once a week.

- Eat one simple meal (soup and salad or soup and sandwich) a week during Lent.

- Collect the money saved from not eating meat or desert and give it to a group in the community or connected to your church that shares food or meals with those in need.

Share. So fasting is giving up or letting go, but it can also be taking up. And sharing or giving to others is a way that children learn about loving God.

- Help kids learn about giving by doing something together. Volunteer to prepare a meal for a homeless shelter.

- Share time with someone who needs a friend or someone who needs help with a simple errand or task at home.

- Connect with a Jewish or Muslim family by sharing a meal. Share some family practices of fasting.

 ### Promises: Parent ClassGathering after a Baptism/Blessing

It is a common practice for churches either to offer a class for parents bringing their children to worship for a baptism or a blessing or for the minister to meet with the parents in the home. Less common is a follow-up with parents after the baptism or blessing. God's spirit present at the baptism or blessing of a child has the possibility of transforming the parent/s, and a reminder about faithfulness to promises is an excellent way to continue table conversations.

Consider offering an annual gathering for parents of children who have been blessed or baptized in worship. Perhaps it could be planned for lunch after church on Sunday or an early meal together in a home on Sunday evening with child care provided. The purpose of such a gathering would be the chance for your church's educator and/or pastor to talk with parents and even extended family members about setting tables of faith in response to the promises made at their child's blessing or baptism. The following discussion questions could be used:

- What have you discovered about the promises you made at your child's baptism or blessing to live the Christian faith and to teach it to your child?

- Who or what has been most helpful to you in supporting and encouraging your faithful parenting of your child?

- In what ways has this congregation been a support for you and your family?

- What memory of your child's baptism or blessing/dedication stands out in your memory?

- As you reflect on your own life of faith, what is your greatest hope for your daughter or son? What do you most want them to learn, experience, and know as a person of faith?

 ### This I Believe—Faith Statement Day at Church

On Pentecost, faithful Christians gathered together seven weeks after Jesus' death and resurrection. Acts 2 tells the story of how suddenly God's spirit rushed in like a huge windstorm and each one started speaking a different language. And they looked at each other wondering what it meant. For a community of believers living on the other side of Easter, Peter's sermon on what we call Pentecost, the birth of the church, reminded them and us of God's promise. God's Spirit, the living presence of God, would pour down on them. "All of them were filled with the Holy Spirit and began to speak in other languages, as the Spirit gave them ability." And then Peter reminded them of the words of the prophet Joel. And he concludes his speech with these words, "Then everyone who calls on the name of the Lord shall be saved."

As a way of marking this special day, provide the opportunity for everyone to write or draw their own faith statement. This could be done as an intergenerational church school class on Pentecost. It could also be done within church school age classes. People could be invited to write, draw, or collage their responses to these questions:

- For younger children: Invite them to draw a picture of God or Jesus or draw a picture in response to the question: What do you like most about church? What is the most important thing God wants us to remember?

- For older children: What story/stories about Jesus do you think it is important to remember? How does God want us to live? Where do you think God's Spirit lives?

- For youth/adults: What is the most important thing the Bible teaches us? What do you believe? What do you think is the most important thing Jesus taught? How would you describe the ways that God wants us to live in this world? I believe . . .

One church that had a faith statement day each year saved the pictures and words that children had made each year and kept them in a folder. These folders were then given to them at their confirmation. They provided a nice way to remember and recall their journey in faith.

John Vest, pastor with youth at Fourth Presbyterian Church in Chicago, involved members of the confirmation class in creating a visual expression of the meaning of their faith by making a faith icon. Icon is the Greek word for image, and Rev. Vest invited each youth to select someone who he or she believes embodies a life of faith. They were reminded that it could be someone from the Bible, someone from their church, someone from their family, one of their friends, or a public figure.

Illustration boards (9″x 12″) were provided for each person to use. Youth were encouraged to think about how they could illustrate something of the life of faith of the person, using pictures, illustrations, or any kind of symbols that would help tell something about the person who being "written" about on the icon. After the icon was completed, it was covered with acrylic mat gel to add a shiny finish. All of the faith icons were displayed for a month in the church so all could see the faith statements created by the youth.

INVITING

One of my nephews is a senior in high school. Like some teenagers you may know, he doesn't like the typical church school learning model for his age group—sitting around a table and talking. But give him something to do, and he's eager to respond. His mother really wanted him to stay connected with church. So Christopher has been teaching in the church school for two years. He is a buddy for a six-year-old with special needs.

Each week he goes to the kindergarten class with Charlie and helps him during the session. When Charlie had to be hospitalized for some tests, Christopher went with his mom to see him. Occasionally he gets invited by parents in the church who have kids with autism spectrum disorders to help out with their birthday parties.

In this commitment of his time and energy, he is living in response to his own baptism and the invitation to living the Christian life that was extended to him at his confirmation. He is helping other kids in the class learn how to interact with Charlie. And he is also learning experientially about special needs kids—how they learn, how they communicate, the ways they grow in their faith. They invite him into their world with their trust in him. And he surrounds them with his strength, his love, and his care for them. Invitations come our way sometimes daily and we choose how to respond.

 ## Inviting Others to Our Table

Help extended family, friends, and faith communities know your beliefs and values and ways to support your commitments. It is important for families who live with the kinds of difference that are described in chapter 3 help others both understand and learn how to support them.

What is normal and everyday for families may not always be understood by others. For example, an interfaith family observing Christian and/or Jewish holy days might not be easily accepted by their immediate families who still wish their grandchildren could be Jewish or Christian (depending upon the grandparent). Or the parents who adopt a child and want that child to learn about his or her birth culture may have to deal with the comments of others who may say, "They're Americans; why does their culture matter now?" The family whose teenage son or daughter comes out to them may encounter intolerant attitudes from friends and coworkers. The committed couple of two mothers or two dads who are parents know in whose homes they are welcome and in whose they are not.

Consider these questions for your own reflection:

1. What is your story? What do you want family and friends to know about your decision to adopt or to be an interfaith couple, raising your child/children in one faith and not the other?

2. When family comes to visit or you go to visit family or friends, is there anything that is essential for them to know about your family? For example: dietary restrictions if you are Jewish or Muslim; how to greet and interact with your kid if he or she has ADD/ADHD or one of the autism spectrum disorders.

3. What holidays, holy days, and family celebrations are important to your family and how do you want family and friends to participate in them? For example, what kinds of books are appropriate gifts for an interfaith family who are raising their kids as Jews or as Christians? If you have adopted your child or children, is their adoption date one you want to remember?

4. How do we talk with our children and how do we keep family and friends informed? Families who know they are different from others in the community or culture not only live with these realities on a daily basis, they also deal with the questions and curiosities and sometimes misinformation of others.

The stories in chapter 3 are illustrations of some of the ways that parents are being honest and direct about their kids and with their kids.

Keeping extended family members, friends, and faith communities "in the loop" about how you talk with your kids about their adoption, or their faith tradition, or how they will develop and learn as a kid with special needs is important and essential. Families who love their teenager who realizes she/he is gay/lesbian/transgendered also know that it is important to listen to their child and her or his requests about if and how this information is shared with others.

How can we help our friends and families understand about the choices we have made and the values, belief, and theology that are behind our decisions? The stories told by the parents and young adults in chapter 3 reveal the deep faith and theological commitments embedded in their thoughts and actions. Sometimes all parents need is for someone to ask:

- Why and how did you make your decision?
- What has been the hardest thing you have experienced?
- What is the best thing about being your family?
- What has been the greatest surprise?
- What do you know now that you wish you had known at the beginning?
- What is the most important thing you want your families, friends, and faith community to know about your family?

 ## Invitation to Support Groups

Some parents of differently abled kids appreciate the church providing some structure for a support group where they can gather once a month for discussion and sharing of concerns. Providing the chance to talk with others who have kids who are mentally or physically challenged is a very concrete way churches can live out the commitments they have promised to families at the baptism/blessing of children. Parents in one church have named their group ESP (Especially Supportive Parents).

Topics for discussion could be decided by the group. An invitation to the pastor and church educator to participate occasionally is helpful in keeping church staff appraised about needs of kids and families.

 ## Marks of Inviting Congregations

What is it about a church that makes you feel welcome? Often it's the way you and your family are greeted when you walk in the door. Sometimes the welcome is made clear in worship. All churches want to grow and be places of welcome for persons seeking a church home. This book is written to challenge some of our assumptions about whom we welcome, whom we invite to the tables we set in our congregations. Consider these best practices of welcome and hospitality. Church committees or ministries such as education/nurture or mission can support the kinds of difference and diversity discussed in this book in several different ways.

Welcoming Words. Look over these mission statements and words of welcome found on church websites. Compare them with your congregation. How are they alike or different?

We welcome you to join us in our journey of faith, regardless of age, race, gender, sexual orientation, economic or family status, ethnic background, and mental or physical abilities. (Second Presbyterian Church, Nashville, Tennessee; secondpresbyterian.net)

San Marino Congregational United Church of Christ is an Open and Affirming church. We affirm the rich complexity of God's creation, which includes every person and many forms of family. We welcome into our open communion and community God's beloved children of all ethnicities, nationalities, ages, genders, sexual orientations, physical or mental limitations, economic and family circumstances, and faith backgrounds. We affirm and celebrate all loving and committed relationships. We commit ourselves to the defense of the spiritual, civic, and human rights of all people, and to the promotion of their well being in our Church and communities. (San Marino Congregational United Church of Christ, San Marino, California; http://www.sanmarinoucc.org/)

Welcome to the Union Church of Lake Bluff! At the Union Church, Christians of different backgrounds gather, with respect for our differences, with compassion for those in need, and with the deep desire to discover God's presence and God's calling in our lives. We're glad that you are visiting! The Union Church is an all denominational church family. We worship the God of grace and love who is revealed in the life, death, and resurrection of Jesus Christ. We believe that, in the end, the God who loves us in this life will love us beyond this life. Because God loves, we seek to love one another, working to see the face of God in every person. Because God is gracious, we seek to be a source of grace in the lives of others, responding to their needs, whether those needs are concrete or spiritual in nature. Because God's love is open to all, we are open to every person who enters our doors. Together, we seek to be the church that God is calling us to be—caring for one another, reaching beyond ourselves, humbly seeking to make a difference in today's world. We invite you to join us, to come as you are and discover the joy of growing in God's grace. (Union Church of Lake Bluff, Illinois; http://www.uclb.org/)

Welcome to Pilgrim Congregational United Church of Christ in Oak Park, Illinois! We're happy you found us! We've been waiting to tell you our story and to show you what Pilgrim Church has to offer. You may be looking for a community who welcomes you as you are. You may be asking how a 2,000-year-old religion could still feel vibrant and be relevant. You may be looking for a church community to help nurture your child. There are many reasons to visit Pilgrim. There are even more reasons to stay. Pilgrims don't all look alike or think alike or act alike. Here you are not required to leave your questions at home or come whole and happy. You are simply invited. Come . . . and listen to the words of Jesus. Come . . . and know God's welcome. Come . . . be a part of real life solutions to real life problems. No matter who you are or where you are on life's journey, you are welcome here . . . at Pilgrim (Pilgrim Congregational United Church of Christ; http://www.pilgrimoakpark.com/)

We welcome everyone! We hope you will visit the Hills Church on a Sunday morning so you can find what we've found: a church that loves God and is committed to welcoming all and healing our broken world; a church full of people who care about you. We are a church of joyful music and exciting ideas, a church that can be home to your faith and your questions. (Wellesley Hills Congregational Church, Wellesley Hills, Massachusetts; http://www.hillschurch.org/)

Imagine a place where children are loved, elders are respected; imagine a place where being different is not considered a deficiency. . . . We are a congregation which is Unashamedly Black and Unapologetically Christian. . . . Our roots in the Black religious experience and tradition are deep, lasting, and permanent. We are an African people, and remain "true to our native land," the mother continent, the cradle of civilization. God has superintended our pilgrimage through the days of slavery, the days of segregation, and the long night of racism. It is God who gives us the strength and courage to continuously address injustice as a people, and as a congregation. We constantly affirm our trust in God through cultural expression of a Black worship service and ministries which address the Black Community. (Trinity United Church of Christ, Chicago, Illinois; http://www.trinitychicago.org/)

Welcoming Worship. How is a welcome made clear in worship? Scan your worship bulletin to see how this is made explicit. Central Presbyterian Church in Atlanta used this call to worship in liturgy during Lent.

The season of Lent is a way that the church marks the holy ground on which we walk when we follow the crucified and risen Jesus. I welcome you to Central today and pray that you will discover something new about what it means for you to be a disciple of Jesus. These baptismal waters claim us all, Asian, African, Latino, Caucasian, gay, straight, bullish on the economy or having been bulldozed by the economy, conservative, progressive, young, younger, and youngest. I am so glad that you are here this morning so that we can lift our voices together in prayer and praise to the throne of God.

Welcoming Space. How is the invitation to your church made explicit in its physical space?

Are the learning spaces for children accessible and safe for all kinds of kids?

If there is a playground, is it accessible to both kids who walk and climb and kids in chairs or with walkers?

Consider walking through your church space with the parent of a kid who is differently abled and see it through their eyes. What changes need to be made?

Welcoming Education. As a Christian Education/Nurture Committee or Ministry, review the goals you have identified for growth in the life of faith for children and youth. Dan Aleshire has written: "Christian education involves those tasks and expressions of ministry that enable people: to learn the Christian story, both ancient and present; to develop the skills they need to act out their faith; to reflect on that story in order to live self-aware to its truth; to nurture the sensitivities they need to live together as a covenant community. (Aleshire 1988)

In addition to these four components I would add one more: Christian education enables learners of all ages to be conversation partners with people of faith traditions different from their own. Now review this list and discuss how each of these goals could be made more specific in light of the reality of living in a world of difference and diversity.

TAKING TIME

Multitasking has become the norm in our culture. It's always better to be doing two things at the same time, talking on the phone *and* driving, texting *and* eating. We seem to have evolved into a culture where singular focus on one activity is not valued. Are we losing the ability to have sustained focus on one thing? Some educators write about how media and social networking are affecting learning and the prevalence of learners exhibiting "constant partial attention." Perhaps you have noticed it in worship or when you are with friends, the people who simply can't *not* check their smart phone.

Yet there are age groups within our culture who need our focused attention and our time: children and older adults. You can't hurry a two-year-old and you can't hurry an elderly adult. You can't! When you are with them, you have to leave your own time zone and get into theirs. After the shock of withdrawal from the fast pace and multi-tasking, you begin to get into their rhythm. And if you allow yourself, you can begin to let yourself like it, this slowing down, this taking time. As a spiritual practice, we can choose to live less by chronos (clock time) and live more by kairos (God's time).

 ### Reading the Bible with Children

Taking time to read a Bible story with a child is a wonderful way to close the day. Good Bible storybooks are in great abundance. Here is a list of my favorites (the last two are more art than story oriented but are great to use with kids). Many are available in local bookstores or all can be ordered from your favorite online bookstore. When family members want suggestions for a gift for your child, give them one of these titles!

1. *The Family Story Bible*, Ralph Milton (Westminster/John Knox Press, 1996).

2. *Lectionary Story Bible, Years A, B, C,* Ralph Milton (Wood Lake Books, 2009). Great for younger children.

3. *CEB Children's Bible* (Abingdon Press, 2012). This is a study Bible for children ages 8–13 based on a completely new translation of the Bible, the Common English Bible, which will be available in fall of 2011.

4. *The Pilgrim Book of Bible Stories,* NRSV (Pilgrim Press, 2003).

5. *Children's Illustrated Bible* (DK Publishing, 1994). Great for elementary age children.

6. *The Bible for Children* (Good Books, 2002).

7. *Bible Storybook*, CEV (American Bible Society, 1990).

8. *Tomie de Paola's Book of Bible Stories*, NIV (Puffin Books, 1990).

9. *The Bible: A People Listen to God* (Liturgical Press, 1998).

10. *The Bible Story,* illustrated by Brian Wildsmith (Oxford University Press, 1989).

11. *Augsburg Story Bible* (Augsburg, 1992).

12. *Children's Bible*, NRSV (Abingdon, 2006).

13. *Art Works of He Qi* (Chinese Christian Literature Council, 1999).

14. *The Bible through Asian Eyes,* Masao Takenaka and Ron O'Grady (Pace Publishing, 1991).

When reading the Bible with children, keep these things in mind:

- Choose the version carefully. Are you using a children's storybook, a children's Bible, or a collection of biblical stories selected for this age group? Know what you are reading from and why you chose it. For example, Ralph Milton has written *The Family Story Bible* and three volumes of *The Lectionary Story Bible*. His story-telling style can best be described as expanded biblical narratives. He goes outside the text, much like a Jewish midrash style of biblical interpretation.

- Engage the story yourself before reading or discussing it with children or youth.

- Use open-ended questions to engage them with the story. For example: Why do you think this story is in the Bible?

- Help them connect with the context—the original audience who heard this story.

- Invite reflection on their connection with the story—begin questions with why or what do you think?

 ### Taking Time and Making Meaning

Consider offering a short subject class for parents with the title "Spiritual Practices for Busy Parents." Or it could be put on a church website or perhaps even printed on a laminated book mark. As parents balance their lives at home and work and manage all the family commitments, it's often common that time for spiritual practices gets lost. This list is not meant to be exhaustive, rather suggestive. What else can you add?

1. Practice the Examen at the end of your day. Where did you see or receive God's love today? Where did you give God's love today?

2. Reread the biblical texts used in worship on Sunday sometime during the week.

3. Pray with your child at the end of the day.

4. Check in with your teenager before you go to bed. In her book *Girl Talk/God Talk,* Joyce Mercer writes about the mother who checked in with her daughter each evening by asking her, "Is there anything keeping you from putting the day to rest?" (Mercer 2008, 11)

5. Take time to notice something in God's world—a bird, a flower, a sunset, a star or moon, or fireflies on a summer night. Say a brief prayer of thanksgiving.

6. Read a psalm. There are all kinds—joy and thanksgiving, praise and lament.

7. Try the ancient spiritual practice of reading scripture, Lectio Divina. Read a biblical text three times with these questions for reflection:

   ▪ After the first hearing, what word jumps out?

   ▪ After the second hearing, what image comes to mind?

   ▪ After the third hearing, how is God speaking to you through this text today?

8. As you feed your baby, name the family members that surround her and give thanks for their presence in her life.

9. Bake some bread and give it away.

10. When you're having a difficult day, practice saying this assurance of God's love and presence in your life: "Goodness is stronger than evil. Love is stronger than hate. Light is stronger than darkness. Life is stronger than death. I believe the good news of Jesus' gospel."

11. Bake some cookies with your son and deliver them together to someone you know.

12. Say a blessing at mealtime, even if it's really short and really fast!

 Giving Bibles or Bible Storybooks

Churches like to give Bibles to children and youth. Some do this at second or third grade when children's reading skills are developed. Many give Bibles to youth at the beginning or end of confirmation or as a graduation present. Some churches like to give children's Bible storybooks to parents of younger children at their birth or adoption. In making decisions about what to give, those on the Education/Nurture Committee should consider these criteria:

- Content—which books, stories are included/omitted? How much is included from the Hebrew Bible and how much from the New Testament?

- Readability—is it easily understood, accessible to the age of the child?

- Is there a good balance between stories about male and female characters?

- For a children's Bible, which translation is used?

- Organization, ease of use—is there help for parents?

- Layout and appropriateness for reader—how much of the story is told?

- Art—in what ways do the illustrations contribute to the story?

 Take Time to Think about VBS

Consider offering an intergenerational evening VBS for four nights that would focus on world religions. One church has called this R and R (Reflection and Renewal) and offered it Sunday through Wednesday nights, 5:30–7:30 or 6:00–8:00 A schedule could work like this:

5:30–6:00 Meal, all together

6:00–7:15 Class options for elementary children, youth, and adults. Preschool kids would have their own separate classes. And a nursery would be provided.

7:15–7:30 Evening prayer

Theme: World Religions. Focus on one faith tradition each evening: Judaism, Islam, Hinduism, Buddhism. The meal could be coordinated so as to reflect foods that would be related to the countries or tables of the religions. Classes would meet Sunday, Monday, and Tuesday. Wednesday evening would be a World Religions Festival, providing the opportunity for each class to present something from their learning experience to the whole group.

In their children's book *How Do You Spell God? Answers to the Big Questions from around the World,* Rabbi Marc Gellman and Monsignor Thomas Hartman have these chapter titles, which would be great titles for classes for this VBS experience: What Question Does Each Religion Want to Answer the Most? Who are the Big Teachers? Where are the Holy Places? When are the Holy Days? (Gellman 1995)

Classes could be offered on the following topics:

- Sacred Texts—Hearing and reading from sacred texts: Koran, Hebrew Bible, the Veda (Hindu) and Sutra (Buddha's teachings).

- Music—Listening to music used in each religion.

- Storytelling—A storyteller could be prepared to tell a story from each religious tradition. An excellent resource is Cherry Gilchrist and Helen Cann's book, *A Calendar of Festivals, Celebrations from around the World,* (Barefoot Books, 1998).

- Holy Days and Rituals—Learn about some of the celebrations and holy days of each of these religions. In addition to the book mentioned above, check out YouTube videos and the Web for visual images.

- Prayer/Movement—Experiencing prayer traditions or movements. This would be another place to invite a guest teacher who is Buddhist, Hindu, Muslim, or Jewish. Have symbols from each tradition available: prayer rug, mala (Buddhist prayer beads), loaf of challah, incense and a bowl of flowers (used by Hindus for daily Puja).

- This I Believe—conversation with a guest who is Jewish, Muslim, Hindu, or Buddhist.

- Words to Know Games—design crossword puzzles or a game using words that are important to know for each of these four faith traditions. For example: Pujah and Dharma, menorah and Sabbath, Buddha and the wheel of life, Allah and Maghrib. An excellent resource is Carolyn Pogue's *A World of Faith, Introducing Spiritual Traditions to Teens,* (Cooper House, 2007).

- Movie—View YouTube clips about these religions. Order DVDs such as *Religions of the World* (six DVD set available for $99.00 from PBS.org) or see what is available in your local public library.

- Cooking—Each evening cook something simple representing each religion. For example: sheera (eaten on the first day of Dwali, the Festival of Lights—Hindu); lentil salad (Muslim); Buddhist tofu soup; Rosh Hashanah honey cookies (Jewish). Recipes like this can be easily located with a Web search.

- Art Activities—connecting with the religion through art. Make prayer flags (Buddhism); Holi (Festival of Colors) paper art or rangoli designs for the Festival of Lights (Hindu); Pillars of Islam or prayer rug (Muslim); Chanukah/Shabbat challah cover (Jewish). Instructions for all of these and other art activities are available on crayola.com.

As you can see, practices of faith are truly the ordinary stuff of life. They are the things we can make commitments to in our families and in our congregations. In considering the ways we invite and are invited; the tables we set and the tables that welcome us; the blessings we give and the blessings we receive; the table conversations that we must have; the choices we make; and the time we take with others and for our own lives of faith—all of these practices tangle us up with God's work of justice, mercy, and kindness.

LEADER'S GUIDE

For those interested in using this book in discussion groups in the church, the following questions will help get you started.

CHAPTER ONE: GOD WHO INVITES

Some general questions that could be used in discussion of this chapter:

1. How have you experienced God's goodness? What has been most satisfying, challenging, disturbing? What new theological tastes have you acquired? Where do you struggle, what questions do you have? Of what are you most sure, "This I Believe"? What are the things that you were most sure about and that now you call into question?

2. On page 4, the Bible is described as a "lens through which we can look and see the world in all of its difference." What is the lens through which you read the Bible?

3. In what ways do you use the Bible at home, both for yourself and with your children?

4. What do you think about the quote by Dr. Cynthia Campbell on page 3, when she says "The Bible is not a book of theology in the sense of being a logical or orderly reflection on the nature of God."

5. Are there other texts with which you wrestle as a Christian living in a world of diversity of faith and culture?

Each of the texts that are examined in this chapter could be used in a Bible study with a group using the following questions:

1. What does this text teach you about living with difference, connecting across ages, culture, race, and theological traditions?
2. What new ways of seeing a familiar Bible story have been opened up for you?
3. What are some ways you could read or tell this story to children and youth? What is the most important thing you want them to hear in this story?
4. Use the questions on page 5 for discussion of each text.

CHAPTER TWO: TABLES WE SET

1. Read the quotes by Eboo Patel and Cynthia Campbell in this chapter. What conversations do we need to be having as communities of faith—about difference and diversity, both within our communities and across communities that are different from ours?
2. Discuss your own responses to the questions at the beginning of the chapter:
   - What happens when we "skate over" the issue of faith?
   - What does it mean to be firmly committed both to your own faith tradition and to interfaith cooperation?
   - What are we called to question and what are we called to affirm? What are we called to reexamine, relearn, rethink as we live into being Christian in a religiously plural culture?
   - In light of what we know now, what does faithfulness to God look like?
3. What experiences of dealing with religious pluralism or interculturalism have you had? What questions have your children asked?

4. Campbell describes three Christian approaches to religious diversity: exclusivism, inclusivism, and pluralism, which are illustrated in the responses to the liturgy for the Presentation of a Child: "There are three Christian approaches to religious diversity and they could have all been present that day: the child is not Christian, she is not baptized, she is outside the church (exclusivist); or her faith is in God's hands (inclusivist); or her life is enriched by growing up with faithful parents who will help her learn about God from two different faith perspectives, Jewish and Christian (pluralist)."

   In what ways is your understanding about God, your theology, impacted by your cultural location? Who are your conversation partners? In what ways are your questions of faith supported or challenged by others?

5. A number of questions are raised at the beginning of this chapter. What others would you add? What in this chapter challenges and confirms some of your own thinking about living in a pluralistic culture?

6. Test your own religious literacy. For example:

   - What are the Ten Commandments and where can you find them?
   - What is the difference between Sunni and Shi'a Islam?
   - What is Ramadan and when does it occur?
   - What is the name of the holy book of Islam?
   - What is Passover? When and how is it observed?

   More questions like these can be found on the web using the words "religious literacy." Take the religious literacy quiz used by Stephen Prothero in his book *Religious Literacy* (HarperSanFrancisco, 2007). With others in the church, discuss the building blocks of world religions that need to be added to strengthen your religious literacy.

7. Review the affirmations that were made in the liturgy for the Presentation of a Child. Where do you see them being affirmed and lived in your congregation?

8. The quote from Rabbi Sandy Eisenberg Sasso encourages individuals to explore "the places they come from." What in your religious tradition has prepared you to live in a pluralist culture? Where do you struggle with the stories of diversity described in this chapter?

9. If your church shares space with another worshiping congregation, what opportunities are there for learning about each other?

10. How do the tables around which you gather in your congregation reveal your response to God who loves us, God who knows us each by name, God who blesses all God's children? Whose place card needs to be added? Who is not on the invitation list?

CHAPTER 3: BLESSINGS

1. Whose baptism do we recognize? In what ways do we affirm and live out of the belief that the waters of baptism claim us all? How is that evidenced in your congregation?

2. Who is welcome at the table?

3. On page 63, the quote from Nancy Ammerman reminds us of the importance of telling stories of faith. What stories of faith emerge from your congregation?

4. Discuss the questions raised on page 64:
   - How is my life blessed by living with diversity?
   - In what ways is living with difference a challenge for me?
   - In what ways is my church a place of welcome for all of God's children? What are the issues of difference that our church still needs to address?
   - What do I need to know, learn, hear, and experience so I will better understand how to live with the diversity present in the communities of which I am a part?

5. In Kienan's story about coming out as a gay teenager, he says that he always felt welcomed and included in church and in the youth group. In what ways is your church supporting parents of LGBT

youth? How are teachers, pastors, and leaders of youth trained to pastorally care for LGBT teenagers?

6. What forms does your church school have for parents to use to provide information about their children and any special needs—medical, dietary, social/interactive, psychological?

7. Read and discuss the story of the Fourth Avenue Presbyterian Church's Sunday school of several faiths. As you discuss it, note places of affirmation, questions, and places where you disagree.

8. This chapter tells stories of differences of culture, faith, sexuality, abilities, and families. Which of these differences are represented in your church? In what ways does your congregation welcome and affirm children, youth, and families? Are there any barriers to their participation in the life of your congregation? Read the contemporary version of the Beatitudes at the end of the chapter and discuss your response to it.

Reference List

INTRODUCTION

Patel, E. 2007. *Acts of Faith.* Boston: Beacon.

CHAPTER ONE

Boring, M. E. 1995. *The New Interpreter's Bible, Vol. 8.* Nashville: Abingdon.

Boring, M. E., and F. Craddock. 2009. *The People's New Testament Commentary.* Louisville: Westminster John Knox.

Campbell, C. 1997. "Follow the Leader," *The Sunday Evening Club,* April 28, http://textweek.com (accessed April 26, 2010).

Campbell, C. 2007. *A Multitude of Blessings: A Christian Approach to Religious Diversity.* Lousiville: Westminster John Knox Press.

Carter, Warren. 2003. In W. Harrelson, ed. *The New Interpreter's Study Bible.* Nashville: Abingdon.

Coles, R. 1990. *The Spiritual Life of Children.* Boston: Houghton Mifflin.

Common English Bible. 2011. Nashville: Abingdon.

Craddock, F. 1990. *Luke.* Interpretation: A Bible Commentary for Preaching and Teaching. Louisville: John Knox Press.

Craddock, F. 2009. *Luke.* Interpretation A Bible Commentary for Teaching and Preaching. Louisville: Westminster/John Knox Press.

Craven, T. 2003. "The Psalms." In W. Harrelson, ed. *The New Interpreter's Study Bible.* Nashville: Abingdon.

Farmer, Kathleen Robertson. 2003. "Ruth." In W. Harrelson, ed. *The New Interpreter's Study Bible.* Nashville: Abingdon.

Frankel, E. 2009. *JPS Illustrated Children's Bible.* Philadephia: Jewish Publication Society.

Fretheim, T. E. 1994. "The Book of Genesis." *The New Interpreter's Bible, Vol. 1.* Nashville: Abingdon Press.

Gellman, M. 1996. *God's Mailbox: More Stories about Stories in the Bible.* New York: Beech Tree.

Green, Joel B. 2003. In W. Harrelson, ed. *The New Interpreter's Study Bible.* Nashville: Abingdon.

Harrelson, W., ed. 2003. *The New Interpreter's Study Bible.* 12 vols. Nashville: Abingdon.

Hiebert, T. 2003. "Genesis." In W. Harrelson, ed. *The New Interpreter's Study Bible*. Nashville: Abingdon.

Hiebert, T. Summer 2007. "God's Plan for Community." *APCE Advocate.*

Hiebert, T., and E. Caldwell. 2008. God's Big Plan.

Milton, R. 2007. *Lectionary Story Bible*. Kelowna, BC, Canada: Wood Lake Books.

Milton, R. 2008. *Lectionary Story Bible Year B*. Kelowana, BC, Canada: Wood Lake Books.

Milton, R. 2009. *Lectionary Story Bible Year C*. Kewlona, BC, Canada: Wood Lake Books.

Nelson, R. D. 1987. *First and Second Kings.* Interpretation: A Bible Commentary for Teaching and Preaching. Louisiville: John Knox Press.

Sakenfeld, K. D. 1999. *Ruth.* Interpretation: A Bible Commentary for Teaching and Preaching. Louisville: John Knox Press.

Sanderson, Judith. 2003. "Micah." In W. Harrelson, ed. *The New Interpreter's Study Bible*. Nashville: Abingdon.

Sasso, S. E. 2007. *God's Echo: Exploring Scripture with Midrash.* Brewster, MA: Paraclete.

Seow, C. L. 1999. "The First and Second Books of Kings." *The New Interpreter's Bible, Vol. 3.* Nashville: Abingdon.

Torre, M. A. 2009. "Luke 19:2–10." *The Peoples' Bible.* Minneapolis: Fortress.

Willimon, W. 1988. *Acts.* Interpretation: A Bible Commentary for Teaching and Preaching. Atlanta: John Knox Press.

CHAPTER TWO

Aja-Sigmon, D. 2010. Interview by E. Caldwell. June 1.

Block, D. 2010. In J. E. Small. *Proclaiming the Great Ends of the Church: Mission and Ministry for Presbyterians.* Louisville: Geneva.

Buchanan, J. 2006. Presentation of a Child. July 16.

Calvin, J. 1960. *Institutes of the Christian Religion.* Ed. J. T. McNeill. Philadelphia: Westminster Press. 4.17.38.

Campbell, C. M. 2007. *A Multitude of Blessings: A Christian Approach to Religious Diversity.* Louisville: Westminster John Knox.

Chittister, J. 2004. *Called to Question.* Lanham, MD: Sheed and Ward.

Forbes, J. 2010. PBS.org. Interview by Tavis Smiley, January 28. http://www.pbs.org/kcet/tavissmiley/archive/201001/20100128.html (accessed February 23, 2010).

Jethani, S. 2009. "Can We Cooperate with Other Faiths without Losing Our Identity?" Skyebox, October 26. http://www.skyejethani.com/ (accessed February 23, 2010).

Levine, A. J. (2006). *The Misunderstood Jew: The Church and the Scandal of the Jewish Jesus.* San Francisco: Harper.

Marty, M. 1993. Christian Education in a Pluralistic Culture. In D. Schuller, *Rethinking Christian Education,* 23. St. Louis: Chalice Press.

Newman, E. 2007. *Untamed Hospitality: Welcoming God and Other Strangers.* Grand Rapids: Brazos Press.

Patel, E. 2007. *Acts of Faith: The Story of an American Muslim, The Struggle for the Soul of a Generation.* Boston: Beacon Presss.

Prothero, S. 2007. *Religious Literacy: What Every American Needs to Know—and Doesn't.* San Francisco: Harper.

Sacks, J. 2001. "The Chief Rabbi's New Year Message—BBC Online Religion and Ethics." September 9. http://www.chiefrabbi.org/CR_ROSH_HASHANA.aspx (accessed March 4, 2011).

Sacks, J. 2002. *The Dignity of Difference: How to Avoid the Clash of Civilizations.* New York: Continuum.

Sasso, S. E. 2006. "Spirituality of Parenting." *Speaking of Faith.* http://speakingoffaith.publicradio.org/programs/spiritualityofparenting/index.shtml (accessed March 15, 2007).

Smith, D. J. 2009. *If America Were a Village: A Book about the People of the United States.* Toronto: Kids Can Press.

Tierney, D. 2004. Coveting Luke's Faith. *The New York Times Magazine,* January 11.

CHAPTER THREE

Ammerman, N. 2006. Journeys of Faith. In James L. Heft, *Passing on the Faith, Transforming Traditions for the Next Generation of Jews, Christians, and Muslims.* New York: Fordham University Press.

Beasley, V. 2010. Interview by E. Caldwell. July 27.

Browning, R. L., and R. A. Reed. 1995. *Models of Confirmation and Baptismal Affirmation: Liturgical and Educational Designs.* Birmingham: Religious Education Press.

Bullock, B. 2010. Interview by E. Caldwell. March.

Caldwell, E. F. 2000, 2007. *Making a Home for Faith: Nurturing the Spiritual Life of Your Children.* Cleveland: Pilgrim Press.

Crawford, D. 2007. Interview by E. Caldwell. April.

Finley, Kristie. 2010. Interview by E. Caldwell. March 22.

Finley, Kienan. 2010. Interview by E. Caldwell. March 21.

Fourth Avenue Presbyterian Church. 2010. "Who We Are." http://fourthavenuepresbyterian.org (accessed May 2010).

Haugen, M. 1994. All Are Welcome. Chicago, IL: GIA.

Janda, J. 1984. *Julian: A Play Based on the Life of Julian of Norwich.* Boston: Seabury Press.

Kapp, D. 2010. Interview by E. Caldwell. March 17.

McCabe, K. 2010. Interview by E. Caldwell. June 27.

Newman, B. J. 2006. *Autism and Your Church: Nurturing the Spiritual Growth of People with Autism Spectrum Disorders.* Grand Rapids: Faith Alive Christian Resources.

Second Presbyterian Church. 2010. Worship bulletin, March 14. Nashville, Tennessee.

Sonnabend, R. 2010. Interview by E. Caldwell. January 24.

Sue. 2010. Interview by E. Caldwell. March 20.

Turnage, L. 2010. Interview by E. Caldwell. March 11.

Weeks, L. 2010. Interview by E. Caldwell. January 29.

Yamada, F. 2010. Interview by E. Caldwell. March 16.

CHAPTER FOUR

Aleshire, D. 1988. "Finding Eagles in the Turkey's Nest: Pastoral Theology and Christian Education." *Review and Expositor* 85, 699.

Bass, D. 2010. *Practicing Our Faith: A Way of Life for a Searching People.* Rev. ed. San Francisco: JosseyBass.

Brooks, J. 2004. *A World of Prayers.* Grand Rapids: Eerdmans Books for Young Readers.

Dykstra, C. 1999. *Growing in the Life of Faith.* Louisville: Geneva.

Finley, Kienan. 2010. Interview by E. Caldwell. March 21.

Gellman, M., and T. Hartman. 1995. *How Do You Spell God?* New York: Morrow.

Halliday, A. 2007. "Creating anti-racist educational communities." *APCE Advocate.* Summer.

International Ecumenical Caucus. 2001. Statement at the U.N. World Conference Against Racism, Racial Discrimination, Xenophobia and Related Intolerance. Durban, South Africa. September 5. The full text can be found at http://www.ncccusa.org/publicwitness/ecumenical caucus.html.

Jensen, D. H. 2010. Adopted into the Family: Toward a Theology of Parenting. *Journal of Childhood and Religion,* 14.

Lewison, Martin. n.d. Plot summary for *Crash.* The Internet Movie Database. http://www.imdb.com/title/tt0375679/plotsummary (accessed July 31, 2010).

Mercer, J. A. 2008. *Girltalk/Godtalk: Why Faith Matters to Teenage Girls— and Their Parents.* San Francisco: Jossey-Bass.

Pilgrim Congregational United Church of Christ, Oak Park, IL. Mission/welcome statement. http://www.pilgrimoakpark.com/.

Prothero, S. 2010. *God Is Not One.* New York: HarperOne.

San Marino Congregational United Church of Christ, San Marino, CA. Mission/welcome statement. http://www.sanmarinoucc.org/.

Second Presbyterian Church, Nashville, TN. Mission/welcome statement. http://www.secondpresbyterian.net.

Schoettle, M. 2000. *W.I.S.E. Powerbook.* Burtonsville, MD: The Center for Adoption Support and Education.

Siler, S. 2010. "Whole in the Sight of God." *Music for the Soul.* http://www.musicforthesoul.org (accessed August 5, 2010).

Hartman, T., and M. Gellman. 1995. *How Do You Spell God?* New York: Morrow Junior Books.

Trinity United Church of Christ, Chicago, IL. Mission/welcome statement. http://www.trinitychicago.org.

Union Church of Lake Bluff, IL. Mission/welcome statement. http://www.uclb.org.

United Nations. 1948. "The Universal Declaration of Human Rights." http://www.un.org/en/documents/udhr/index.shtml.

Wellesley Hills Congregational Church, Wellesley Hills, MA. Welcome statement. http://www.hillschurch.org.

Wuthnow, R. 1999. *Growing Up Religious: Christians and Jews and Their Journeys of Faith.* Boston: Beacon.

Resources

This list is not mean to be exhaustive, rather suggestive for the wealth of books and resources that are available both in print and on the web.

BOOKS FOR CHILDREN

Bergen, Lisa Tawn. *God Found Us You.* New York: HarperCollins, 2009.

Campbell, Keri. *Lily.* Charleston, SC: BookSurge, 2009. ISBN 1439213240.

Czech, Jan M. *The Coffee Can Kid.* Washington D.C.: Child and Family Press, 2002.

Parr, Todd. *The Family Book.* New York: Little, Brown, 2003.

Polacco, Patricia. *In Our Mothers' House.* New York: Philomel Books, 2009.

Richardson, Justin. *And Tango Makes Three.* New York: Simon and Schuster, 2005.

Schoettle, Marilyn. *W.I.S.E. Up!* Powerbook. Burtonsville, MD: The Center for Adoption Support and Education, 2000. ISBN:0971173206.

World Religions

Brooks, Jeremy. *A World of Prayers.* Grand Rapids: Eerdmans, 2004.

Gee, Martha Bettis. *Seven Friends, Seven Faiths: Looking at Celebrations of Different Faiths. Teacher's Guide.* New York: General Board of Global Ministries, United Methodist Church, 2003.

Gilchrist, Cherry. *A Calendar of Festivals: Celebrations from around the World.* Cambridge, MA: Barefoot Books, 1998.

Khan, Rukhsana. *Muslim Child: Understanding Islam through Stories and Poems.* Morton Grove, IL: Albert Whitman, 1999.

Madison, Ron. *Ned and the World's Religions, As Seen through the Eyes of Children.* Ron Madison Books, 2007. ISBN 10:1887206264.

Maestro, Betsy, and Giulio Maestro. *The Story of Religion.* New York: Clarion Books, 1996.

Meredith, Susan. *The Usborne Book of World Religions.* London: Usborne Publishing, 1996.

Podwall, Mark. *Jerusalem Sky, Stars, Crosses, and Crescents,* New York: Doubleday, 2005.

Pogue, Carolyn. *A World of Faith: Introducing Spiritual Traditions to Teens.* Kelowna, BC, Canada: Wood Lake Books, 2007.

Simons, Nina, Leslie Swartz, and the Children's Museum, Boston. *Moonbeams, Dumplings & Dragon Boats: A Treasury of Chinese Holiday Tales, Activities, and Recipes.* Orlando: HarcourtBooks, 2002.

Smith, Chris. *One City, Two Brothers.* Cambridge, MA: Barefoot Books, 2007.

Cultural Diversity

Choi, Yangsook. *The Name Jar.* New York: Dell Dragonfly, 2003.

The Milestones Project: Celebrating Childhood around the World. Berkeley: Tricycle Press, 2004.

Milway, Katie Smith. *One Hen: How One Small Loan Made a Big Difference.* Toronto: Kids Can Press, 2008.

Munson, Derek. *Enemy Pie.* Chronicle Books, 2000.

Strauss, Rochelle. *One Well: The Story of Water on Earth,* Toronto: Kids Can Press, 2007.

Smith, David J. *If America Were a Village: A Book about the People of the United States.* Toronto: Kids Can Press, 2009.

————. *If the World Were a Village.* Toronto: Kids Can Press, 2002.

Winter, Jeanette. *The Librarian of Basra: A True Story from Iraq.* New York: Harcourt, 2005.

————. *Wangari's Trees: A True Story from Africa,* New York: Harcourt, 2008.

Faith

Buller, Laura. *A Faith Like Mine: A Celebration of the World's Religions—Seen through the Eyes of Children.* New York: DK Publishing, 2005.

Children's Mission Yearbook for Prayer and Study. Louisville: Witherspoon Press, 2010. ISBN 978571530981. Although this book is written for a Presbyterian audience, the educational activities related to mission and service for kids are easily adaptable in other faith denominations.

Jelenek, Frank X. *Journey to the Heart: Centering Prayer for Children.* Brewster, MA: Paraclete Press, 2008.

Lane, Leena. *Angels among Us.* Grand Rapids: Eerdmans, 2007.

Weaver, Lisa. *Praying with Our Feet.* Scottsdale, PA: Herald Press, 2005.

Differently Abled Kids

Elder, Jennifer. *Autistic Planet.* London: Jessica Kingsley, 2007.

Hoopmann, Kathy. *All Cats Have Asperger Syndrome.* London: Jessica Kingsley, 2006.

————. *All Dogs Have ADHD*. London: Jessica Kingsley, 2008.

————. *Blue Bottle Mystery: An Asperger Adventure*. London: Jessica Kingsley, 2001.

Larson, Elaine Marie. *I Am Utterly Unique: Celebrating the Strengths of Children with Asperger Syndrome and High-Functioning Autism*. Overland Park, KS: Autism Asperger Publishing, 2006

Seskin, Steve, and Allen Shamblin. *Don't Laugh at Me*. Berkeley: Tricycle Press, 2002

Wine, Angela. *What It Is to Be Me! An Asperger Kid Book*. Fairdale Publishing, 2005. ISBN 978-1593521998.

Interfaith Families

Hawxhurst, Joan C. *Bubbe & Gram: My Two Grandmothers*. Kalamazoo: Dovetail Publishing, 1996.

Meyer, Michele Lee. *My Daddy Is Jewish and My Mommy Is Christian*. Charleston, SC: BookSurge, 2006.

Older, Effin. *My Two Grandmothers*. New York: Harcourt Children's, 2000.

Bibles, Bible Storybooks

Young Children

Frankel, Ellen, and Avi Katz. *JPS Illustrated Children's Bible*. Philadelphia: Jewish Publication Society of America, 2009.

Milton, Ralph. *Lectionary Story Bible*, Kelowna, BC, Canada: Wood Lake Books, Year A, 2007; Year B, 2008; Year C , 2009.

Older Children

Common English Bible Children's Study Bible. Common English Bible, 2011.

Hastings, Selina. The Children's Illustrated Bible. New York: DK Publishing, 1994.

RESOURCES FOR ADULTS
Books

Campbell, Cynthia. *A Multitude of Blessings*. Louisville: Westminster John Knox, 2007. There is an excellent leader's guide for use in teaching this book available at http://www.ppcbooks.com/wjk_studyguides.asp.

Gruzen, Lee F., and Sheila Gordon. *Raising Your Jewish/Christian Child: How Interfaith Parents Can Give Children the Best of Both Their Heritages*. 2nd ed. New York: Newmarket Press, 2001,

Hawxhurst, Joan C. *The Interfaith Family Guidebook: Practical Advice for Jewish and Christian Partners.* Kalamazoo: Dovetail Publishing, 1998.

Hoekman, Laurel A. *ASD to Z . . . Basic Information, Support, and Hope for Individuals Diagnosed with Autism Spectrum Disorders.* Zeerland, MI: Gray Center for Social Learning and Understanding, 2005.

Newman, Barbara J. *Autism and Your Church: Nurturing the Spiritual Growth of People with Autism Spectrum Disorders.* Grand Rapids, MI: Faith Alive Christian Resources, 2006.

————. *Helping Kids Include Kids with Disabilities.* Grand Rapids, MI: Faith Alive Resources, 2001.

Niebuhr, Gustav. *Beyond Tolerance: Searching for Interfaith Understanding in America.* New York: Viking, 2008.

Notbohm, Ellen. *Ten Things Every Child with Autism Wishes You Knew.* Arlington, TX: Future Horizons, 2005.

————. *Ten Things Your Student with Autism Wishes You Knew.* Arlington, TX: Future Horizons, 2006.

Stevenson-Moessner, Jeanne. *The Spirit of Adoption: At Home in God's Family.* Westminster John Knox, 2003.

Wuthnow, Robert. *America and the Challenges of Religious Diversity.* Princeton, NJ: Princeton University Press, 2005.

Articles

"Children and Spirituality: Live as Children of Light," *Hungry Hearts* 13/1 (Spring 2004). http://www.pcusa.org/spiritualformation/hungryhearts/. Click on archives.

Websites

Busted halo.com. Check out the Lenten calendar, "Fast, Pray, Give." This is a website sponsored by Paulist Fathers and designed as online magazine for young adult spiritual seekers: http://www.bustedhalo.com.

Calendars: Two excellent calendars are great to use with families are "Salt of the Earth: A Christian Seasons Calendar," available from http://www.thechristiancalendar.com/, and "Multifaith Calendar," available each year from the Multifaith Action Society, http://www.multifaithaction.org/.

The Canadian Ecumenical Anti-Racism Network has a great website of resources: http://www.wicc.org/programsevents/Racial_Justice/CEARN.html.

Crayola has a great website for art activities for intergenerational learning: http://www.crayola.com. Look at lesson plans.

Devotional series at http://www.d365.org. Great online Lenten daily meditation.

The Dovetail Institute for Interfaith Family Resources has one of the best websites for information about interfaith families: http://www.dovetailinstitute.org.

Faith Practices is a new (2010) resource from the United Church of Christ. It is an online resource offering educational resources for growing in the life of faith. http://www.Faithpractices.org.

Theholidayspot.com. Great resource for learning about holidays celebrated by all religions: http://www.theholidayspot.com/.

Musicforthesoul.org. Great musical resources for faith, families, and children relating to welcoming all the difference in God's world: http://www.musicforthesoul.org/.

Racism: For resources for workshops dealing with antiracism and white privilege, go to YouTube and look at the following videos by Peggy McIntosh, an educator in California: "Examining the racism we carry"; "Mirrors of Privilege: Making Whiteness Visible," Parts 1, 2, 3; and "Unpacking the Invisible Knapsack."

Speakingoffaith.org. Great website for interviews and resources for faith formation. For more information about "pocket prayers" mentioned in chapter 4, see this posting: http://blog.onbeing.org/post/318645541/my-pocket-prayers.

The Thoughtful Christian is an online resource for studies for adults and youth. It has the following excellent studies available: Buddhism, Introduction to the Koran, Islam, Judaism, Scientology, Shi'ite and Sunis. See http://www.thethoughtfulchristian.com and click on Contemporary Issues—World Religions.

Resource for workshops on faith and religious diversity in PowerPoint format: beliefnet.com, http://religions.pppst.com/world-religions.html.